Medical Toxicology Unit, Guy's & St Thomas' Hospital Trust

Chemical Incident Management for Local Authority Environmental Health Practitioners

Dr Robyn Fairman

Dr Virginia Murray

Dr Alan Kirkwood

Patrick Saunders

London: The Stationery Office

Applications for reproduction should be made in writing to The Stationery Office Limited, St Crispins, Duke Street, Norwich NR3 1PD.

While every effort has been made to ensure that the information contained in this publication is correct at the time of going to press, responsibility for accuracy of the medical content of this book rests solely with its authors and The Stationery Office cannot be held responsible for any errors.

A CIP catalogue record for this book is available from the British Library
A Library of Congress CIP catalogue record has been applied for

First published 2001

ISBN 0 11 322121 5

Books are to be returned on or before
the last date below.

Chemical Incident Management for Accident and Emergency Clinicians

Contents

Appendices

Boxes

Figures

Tables

Contributors

Dr Robyn Fairman is a lecturer in Environmental Health at Kings College in London. Before this she worked as a local authority environmental health practitioner for seven years. Her research interests are the assessment and management of environmental health risk, and she has carried out projects for the European Environment Agency and the United Nations International Register of Potentially Toxic Chemicals.

Dr Virginia Murray, FFOM, FRCP, FRCPath, trained in occupational medicine before joining the National Poisons Information Service, London and the Medical Toxicology Unit which is based at Guy's and St Thomas' Hospital NHS Trust in 1980. Initially she was involved in projects working in the Unit but also assisted in the Unit's collaboration with the International Programme on Chemical Safety (WHO/ILO/UNEP). Since 1988 she has played a key role in developing the Unit's ability to respond to problems arising from chemical incidents. In 1989, she started the Chemical Incident Research Programme at the Unit which in 1996 developed into the Chemical Incident Response Service, of which she is the Director. As a result she has considerable experience in advising on response to chemical incidents.

Dr Alan Kirkwood qualified as an environmental health officer in 1966 and spent 24 years in local government. Since 1990 he has lectured at the Home Office Emergency Planning College, where he was Course Director, and now lectures for the Open University and University of Leicester in environmental management, and crisis and disaster management.

Patrick Saunders is an Environmental Health Officer who has worked in local government, on secondments to the World Health Organisation and the Health Education Council. He was Environmental Health Advisor to the West Midlands Regional Health Authority. He currently works at Birmingham University providing a public health practice service to the Health Authorities in the region, together with a research (especially the health effects of environmental contamination) and a teaching role. He established the West Midlands regional chemical incident surveillance programme. Having been involved with managing several major chemical incidents, he is currently Assistant Director of the Chemical Hazard Management and Research Centre, which provides a 24-hour response service to the West Midlands region.

Series foreword

This handbook is written at the request of environmental health practitioner colleagues to reflect the needs found by them and other professionals who have been working together during the response to chemical incidents.

Chemical incident response is a developing area for local authority environmental health practitioners. The support provided by you and environmental health colleagues is invaluable in contributing to effective and timely chemical incident response.

I am very grateful to Robyn Fairman for having the enthusiasm and dedication to work with us at the Chemical Incident Response Service to take the lead in writing this handbook and for the contributions from the other authors. Thanks are also due to those who have been kind enough to comment both supportively and critically on the drafts of this book.

This book reflects the outlines used in preparing similar books in the Chemical Incident Management Series for public health physicians and accident and emergency clinicians. The purpose of this is to facilitate information and skill sharing between the three professional groups so that they can more easily take part in the response process in an environment which is frequently stressed, requiring rapid and appropriate decision making to minimise harm to the population at risk.

Since the media are likely to be involved in any significant chemical incidents, early collaboration and communication will help the responders. I hope that this handbook will help with this process.

Virginia Murray

Director
Chemical Incident Response Service
Guy's and St Thomas' National Health Service Trust

Foreword

Among the groups of professionals who may be called on to respond to a chemical incident, local authority environmental health practitioners uniquely combine a knowledge of local services, local industry and their local communities. While rarely at the sharp end of a response, such practitioners, with this knowledge, together with their own investigative skills and regulatory experience, nevertheless quickly come into their own support of the emergency services in environmental sampling, risk assessment, risk communication and liaison with other local government services. They may take the lead later, during the recovery phase.

Fortunately, chemical incidents of any size are relatively rare. This means, however, that few environmental health practitioners will ever gain much practical experience of dealing with them. They must be prepared for them, nevertheless, and this guide should help bridge that experience gap, enabling them to plan and, when called on, play their role more effectively.

Howard Price

Assistant Secretary
Chartered Institute of Environmental Health

Acknowledgements

Elinor Battrick, MSc student attached to Chemical Incident Response Service.

Joan Bennett, Personal Assistant to Dr Murray, Chemical Incident Response Service.

Alan Blisset, Environmental Health Manager and Jeanette McAuliffe, Environmental Health Officer, London Borough of Southwark.

E. Clark, Chief Fire Officer, North Yorkshire Fire and Rescue.

John Collins, Head of Environmental Health and Consumer Protection, Torbay Council.

Malcolm Dubber, Scientific Officer, National Focus.

Mike Eastwood, Research Fellow in Public Health and Environmental Health Adviser to NHS Executive NW, Liverpool John Moores University.

Jody Foster, Environmental Health Officer, South West Region.

Richard Harbord, Managing Director, London Borough of Hammersmith and Fulham.

Stephen Hedley, Principal Environmental Health Officer, South East Institute of Public Health.

Alan Higgins, Chief Environmental Health and Trading Standards Officer, Portsmouth City Council.

Steve Humpries, National Human Health Project Manager, Environment Agency.

Howard Price, Assistant Secretary, Chartered Institute of Environmental Health.

Paul Read, Chief Emergency Planning Officer, Tyne and Wear Emergency Planning Unit.

Ken Rose, Chief and Assistant, Chief Fire Officers' Association.

Dr John Simpson, Consultant in Communicable Disease Control, Wiltshire Health Authority.

Marc Willimont, Environmental Health Officer, Herefordshire Council.

Emma Waterworth, Research Assistant, Kings College London.

Members of staff of the Chemical Incident Response Service and the Medical Toxicology Unit, Guy's and St Thomas' Hospital NHS Trust, London.

List of abbreviations

AQS	Air Quality Standards
BESMIC	Bedfordshire Emergency Services Major Incident Committee
CAS	Chemical Abstract Series
CCDC	Consultant in Communicable Disease Control
CEAS	Chemical Emergency Agency Service
CEC	Commission of the European Communities
CEPO	County Emergency Planning Officer
CHEMDATA	Chemical database used by the fire service
CHEMET	Chemical Incident Meteorological Forecasting Service
CHEMSAFE	Chemical Industry Scheme for Assistance in Freight Emergencies
CIRUS	Chemical database used by London Fire Service
CIEH	Chartered Institute of Environmental Health
COMAH	Control of Major Accident Hazards Regulations
COSHH	Control of Substances Hazardous to Health Regulations
CPHM	Consultant in Public Health Medicine
DETR	The Department of the Environment, Transport and the Regions
DH	Department of Health (England and Wales)
DWI	The Drinking Water Inspectorate
EA	Environment Agency
EHP	Environmental health practitioner
EMARC	Environmental Monitoring and Response Centre
EPO	Emergency planning officer
F&CDA	Fire & Civil Defence Authorities
FEPA	Food & Environmental Protection Act
FSA	The Food Standards Agency
GIS	Geographical Information Systems
HAGCCI	Health Advisory Group on Chemical Contamination Incidents
HAZCHEM	Hazardous chemical label
HELA	Health and Safety/Local Authority Enforcement Liaison Committee
HESMIC	Hertfordshire Emergency Services Major Incident Committee

HSE	Health and Safety Executive
HSG	Health Service Guidance
HSWA	Health and Safety at Work Act 1974
ICSC	International Chemical Safety Card
IPC	Integrated Pollution Control
IPCS	International Programme on Chemical Safety(WHO/ILO/UNEP)
IPPC	Integrated Pollution Prevention and Control
LGC	Laboratory of the Government Chemist
MAFF	Ministry for Agriculture, Fisheries & Food
MEL	Maximum Exposure Limit
NAIR	National Arrangements for Incidents involving Radioactivity
NCEC	National Chemical Emergency Centre – part of AEA Technology
NEHAP	National Environmental Health Action Plan
NIEH	Non-infectious Environmental Hazard
NIHHS	Notification of Installations Handling Hazardous Substances Regulations
NIO	Northern Ireland Office
NPIS	National Poisons Information Service
NRPB	National Radiological Protection Board
NTIS	National Teratology Information Service
OEL	Occupational Exposure Level
PPE	Personal Protective Equipment
RDPH	Regional Director of Public Health
RIMNET	Radioactive Incident Monitoring Network
RSPU	Regional Service Provider Units (chemical incident adviser units of NHS)
SCIEH	Scottish Centre for Infection and Environmental Health
SE	Scottish Executive
SEIPH	South East Institute of Public Health
SEPA	Scottish Environment Protection Agency
TREM	Transport Emergency Cards
WA	Welsh Assembly
WHO	World Health Organisation

Introduction

Chemical incidents arise every day. In a recent survey of local authorities in England, Wales and Northern Ireland, nearly 50% of district or unitary authorities had experienced a chemical incident in 1999 (Waterworth and Fairman, 2000). For any one local authority they may be infrequent occurrences, but their impact can be devastating. Local authority environmental health staff have an important part to play in these incidents. As locally based professionals with a wide knowledge and understanding of local services and hazards, environmental health staff can play a crucial role in the initial response to an incident and an important role in the assessment and in the management of follow-up action. An example is the following case study (Box 1) of the involvement of an environmental health service in an asbestos fire.

Box 1 Environmental health involvement in a chemical incident

During the demolition of a building with an asbestos cement roof, the builder made a small fire of demolition materials. The fire got out of control and the whole building went up in flames causing a plume containing asbestos to billow over the surrounding residential area. The fire brigade was first at the scene and notified the Environmental Health Department. The Environmental Health Department dispatched an experienced officer to the site who assisted the fire brigade by providing advice on the degree of risk and health effects. The fire brigade put out the fire and pulled out. It was then the responsibility of the Environmental Health Department to arrange and oversee the clean-up operation. An abatement notice under the Environmental Protection Act 1990 was served on the builder to clean up the debris.

The role of environmental health practitioners (EHPs)[1] in chemical incidents is not clear-cut and in the past there has been little attempt to define clearly the input that they should have in an increasingly important area. There are a number of reasons for this. The nature of work carried out within environmental health services can vary due to the differing political priorities of local authority elected members. Some local authority environmental health services operate mainly through their regulatory functions, carrying out statutory powers and duties. Others are much more proactive in their approach to environmental health, and actively attempt to manage environmental health issues through both regulatory and non-regulatory channels. Either way, environmental health services tend to take a holistic approach to problem solving which highlights their importance when a multi-agency response is required to an incident. The increasing pressures on budgets and competing demands for resources have made the establishment of new procedures which do not have a legislative driver particularly difficult.

Chemical incidents can prompt regulatory responses by local authorities as shown in the case study (Box 2). In many incidents, there may not be clear regulatory

Box 2 A water contamination incident

The Environmental Health Department was notified of a water contamination incident when a resident of a large housing estate complained about 'red' drinking water. The EHP considered that the incident might affect the health of a large number of people and informed the neighbourhood housing officer and the health authority of the incident and potential risks. The EHP then visited the housing estate to determine whether a health risk existed and to identify the numbers of people potentially affected. The EHP established that the residents were being exposed to the contaminated water (i.e. a source–path–receptor linkage existed) and that 70 to 80 people were potentially exposed. The EHP considered that the most likely cause was cross-connection of the central heating supply to the mains supply via a domestic appliance. The EHP advised those affected not to drink the water until notified that it was safe to do so. Supplies of bottled water were provided. Samples of the contaminated water were sent to a laboratory for analysis. The neighbourhood housing officer assisted the EHP in visiting all potentially affected flats to inspect for any cross-connection of domestic appliances with the mains supply and to examine the water supply. The EHP played an important role in identifying the hazard and assessing the risk as well as in giving advice to residents and taking remedial action.

responsibility imposed on the authority, but the role of the local EHPs could be crucial in providing quick, local, knowledgeable advice.

The UK National Environmental Health Action Plan (NEHAP) has the following objective related to Natural Disasters and Nuclear Accidents:

To limit the consequences of natural disasters, prevent the occurrence and limit the consequences of major industrial and nuclear accidents, and ensure the existence of effective arrangements for emergency preparedness for and response to natural and manmade disaster, in and between countries. (DoE/DH, 1996)

NEHAP points out that further work is required to develop the public health response to chemical accidents. Risk assessment, the rapid availability of expert information and advice to those dealing with the incident at a local level, and the consideration of the need for follow-up action were all identified as needing further work.

This book aims to lay down the building blocks that will allow local authority environmental health services to develop procedures at a local level to deal effectively and appropriately with chemical incidents. It is broken into the four stages seen as vital in an integrated management approach to chemical incidents (OECD, 1992; Home Office, 1997):

• Prevention
• Preparedness
• Response
• Recovery

This is likely to be an unfamiliar approach to EHPs dealing with pollution whose work traditionally focuses on 'response', but it is necessary in dealing with chemical incidents. Without prevention and preparedness the response to incidents may be ineffectual, impossible or may pose dangers to those attempting to deal with the incident.

What is a chemical incident?

There is much discussion as to what constitutes a chemical incident. Many local authorities will not see themselves as being involved in a chemical incident because of their perception that incidents are large-scale, major disasters. Of course major disasters will be 'incidents', but so too will a fire emitting toxic fumes, an oil storage tank leaking and polluting the land, or contaminated drinking water resulting from inadequate maintenance of a water storage tank.

A useful definition of a chemical incident is

An event leading to exposure of two or more individuals to any substance resulting in illness or potentially toxic threat to health.

This definition has been modified from one given by Hill and O Sullivan (1992). It encompasses incidents both severe and minor, and covers all the effects of chemicals (toxic and radioactive). It does not distinguish between events that have to be planned for, such as accidental releases from industrial sites regulated under the Control of Major Accident Hazard Sites Regulations 1999, and those that do not, such as an accidental release from a heating oil tank. Using this definition of chemical incident, local authority environmental health services will be involved in chemical incident response. Chemical incidents will not be a frequent occurrence, but environmental health services need to be prepared and able to respond when they do occur.

The primary objective of local authority environmental health services is the protection of the local population from risks to their health arising from the impact of human activities upon the environment. Dealing with chemical incidents clearly comes within this remit but there is confusion as to roles and responsibilities. This is clear from a survey of local authority environmental health services (Waterworth and Fairman, 2000) and from discussions with fire services and others working in the field.

The role of the local authority environmental health staff in chemical incidents may be

- as part of the emergency planning team to make the initial assessment of potential damage to human health or the environment;
- to act as the local first response to an incident and to carry out sampling necessary in the important period just after a release;
- to enforce environmental health legislation, e.g. statutory nuisance provisions, contaminated land control, private water supplies.

Is the response to all incidents the same?

Some incidents will be classed as **major incidents**. These pose a serious threat to the health of the community or the environment. An example of a major incident is a lorry carrying chemicals overturning and the release to ground and water of large amounts of toxic and flammable chemicals. This type of incident will be planned for through the emergency planning process and integrated emergency management and roles and responsibilities will be reasonably clear. The local authority emergency plan may be activated. The local authority may have a part to play in the incident through the provision of alternative housing, advice and support. In addition the environmental health services will have a part to play alongside other agencies involved.

At the other end of the scale there may be incidents that pose little or no threat to health and may cause disturbance or annoyance only. An example could be odour from a fire. Again in such cases, roles and responsibilities will be reasonably clear. If little or no health risk exists, environmental health services will have to consider whether they can intervene in the situation to prevent a statutory nuisance from occurring or continuing.

In the middle of these two extremes we have what we shall refer to as **minor inci- dents**, for example when potentially toxic chemicals in sealed containers are dumped. The health effects are unknown but the potential for damage is great if anyone has access to the chemicals. In such cases, roles and responsibilities are less clear. From the viewpoint of many environmental health services, the location of the chemicals will determine what role they have. This is because they are viewing the problem with their regulatory functions in mind. This is obviously important to ensure both that they perform their functions adequately, and that those who have the legal powers to rectify the problem are contacted. However, from a wider view of protecting the health of the community there is a role for EHPs wherever the chemicals have been dumped. Irrespective of any statutory role for environmental health services, they are often the bodies to whom local residents turn for information. Their role should not be underrated and even when little or no health risk exists the public may still look to the local authority EHP for reas- surance.

---

[1] The term environmental health practitioner refers to any professional acting to control those aspects of the environment with the potential to affect health, e.g. environmental health officers, technical officers, scientific officers etc.

Section One

Prevention

Chemical incident management seeks to identify hazards through surveillance, and to institute appropriate preventive measures. Chemical incidents may be rare events for local authorities, but they cause significant distress to individuals and communities. A rapid and effective response is essential to prevent or minimise chemical exposure which may lead to adverse health effects of acute or delayed onset and distress.

1 Surveillance

Introduction

Prevention from an environmental health perspective will involve three issues:

- the establishment and implementation of a surveillance system that will inform preventive measures;
- the implementation of regulatory and policy frameworks available for the prevention of chemical incidents; and
- the establishment of communication links and liaison arrangements with other bodies.

At present surveillance for chemical incidents is not universal in local authorities. In this section the needs and benefits of surveillance, the local authority experience of incidents and the regulatory frameworks for prevention will be outlined.

What is chemical incident surveillance?

Surveillance is the continuous analysis, interpretation and feedback of systematically collected data (Last, 1982). Chemical incident surveillance describes the nature, range, frequency and effect of incidents, enabling environmental health agencies to respond and plan for them. The identification, collection and analysis of data require resources, expertise and the active participation of several agencies, some of which may not have a tradition in surveillance. There are currently few surveillance systems anywhere in the world. The most developed outside the UK is maintained by the ATSDR in the United States (ATSDR, 1997). If surveillance really is information for action (Palmer, 2000), the agencies contributing or responding to the system must have confidence in the quality of the information. This is particularly important for chemical incidents as formal response mechanisms are in their infancy (certainly in comparison with communicable diseases) and their effectiveness depends upon multi-agency collaboration. It is important to demonstrate to all agencies the value of their participation through the quality of the surveillance product. In addition to the core objective of incident surveillance, an effective system can also be developed to include the routine surveillance of

- potential sources of incidents;
- potentially exposed persons; and
- diseases potentially associated with chemical releases.

While local authorities will have a role to play in these epidemiological studies of health effects of chemical exposures, their primary responsibilities relate to the prevention of and immediate response to incidents. This section accordingly concentrates on these aspects and is based largely on the experiences of establishing and developing the West Midlands programme (Chemical Hazard Management and Research Centre, 1999).

Why is surveillance important?

An effective surveillance system will provide:

- information for developing appropriate public health prevention and response strategies; and
- a database of incidents for follow-up of exposed persons and casualties and for the targeting of further studies.

Surveillance of environmentally related disease, contaminated persons and potential sources of contamination is specifically required of the NHS (Department of Health, 1993) and while incident surveillance is not formally required it is vital in planning for, and responding to, incidents. Local authorities have specific responsibilities for the surveillance of nuisances response to major emergencies and the monitoring of industrial processes. In addition, they may be the first body to receive complaints of an incident and may be the only agency involved in some releases. Local authorities have access to data and expertise critical to an effective surveillance system and are therefore essential participants. In return, surveillance data may enable local authorities to target resources and improve planning.

Chemical incident surveillance systems

A chemical incident surveillance system should collect a minimum dataset on all incidents of interest within a specified geographical area. Participants can include all the agencies that have responsibilities for responding to chemical releases, e.g. local authorities, health authorities, the National Poisons Information Service, the ambulance service, fire services, the Environment Agency, etc.

It is helpful to collect information on incidents that do not lead to significant exposures (equivalent of 'near misses' in health and safety terms) or incidents that do not trigger the major emergency plans. The former provide valuable intelligence on the potential for accidents and many of the latter are actually of public health significance (Fowle et al., 1996). Agreed definitions are therefore extremely important. All the participating agencies must agree and understand what an incident is.

A chemical incident surveillance system requires

- a contact individual in each participating organisation;
- standardised, formal notification procedures. It is possible to reduce the burden for the data provider by agreeing that copies of incident log sheets can be sent periodically (e.g. by the fire service);
- internal quality assurance checks are a vital part of maintaining the system and developing consistency within and between the different regional systems; and
- access to database resources and skills. The resource implications should not be underestimated. An underfunded service will undermine the credibility of the system.

In the West Midlands, the surveillance system is subject to documented procedures and is database driven with internet access. This requires specific details from inputting staff and will not allow an incident to be closed until these are completed. A monitoring committee meets monthly to randomly select and assess incident reports. At a national level, the National Focus coordinates regional systems and routinely checks a subset of participating surveillance programmes (www.natfocus).

The benefits of surveillance

Surveillance of incidents and diseases arising therefrom is sound public health practice and addresses some statutory responsibilities. Intelligence about the nature, frequency, distribution and impact of incidents and sites of significant risk provides confidence that incidents are identified as early as possible, enables public health agencies to prepare for the potential effects of chemical releases and develop appropriate public health prevention and response strategies (including staff training needs) and provides a database of incidents for the follow-up of exposed persons. In addition, as there are several sources of relevant data, the development of an active surveillance system helps build robust relationships with the key agencies.

An effective system will:

- provide information on trends in time, place and persons that help the identification and anticipation of problems including investigative or control measures;
- inform decisions about personal protective equipment and the location of decontamination facilities during site work by local authority and health authority staff;
- provide background data on the location of processes and potentially contaminated sites important for both regulatory and surveillance purposes;
- provide data on chemicals used within and around a district and assist in emergency planning and securing access to appropriate resources; and
- develop a network of participants that can have added value as other initiatives may be triggered. In the West Midlands, the fire services agree to notify the Chemical Hazard Management and Research Centre (an NHS regional chemical incident response service) of any serious incident. This teamwork is particularly important now, as health authorities have a statutory duty to collaborate with local authorities and as public health observatories, with their commitment to real collaboration, begin to develop.

Linking health data to exposure data is a potential benefit of developing incident surveillance. There are several difficulties associated with this, but addressing these brings different disciplines and organisations together to share expertise and resources.

This is an underdeveloped area and the resources to effectively develop and manage a system should not be underestimated. Given this and the need for the coordination of several agencies, it is probably more appropriate for this type of surveillance to be conducted at a regional level. While the specific responsibility for managing the surveillance rests with health authorities, the input of local authorities is essential. In return, local authorities can receive good-quality data on an important public health issue.

Incidents and local authorities – the current position

A recent census of local authorities in England, Wales and Northern Ireland showed that nearly 50% had experienced a chemical incident in 1999

(Waterworth and Fairman, 2000). There was an average of 2.8 incidents per authority in those authorities that had experienced an incident, and 1.3 incidents when averaged over all the local authorities that responded. This suggests that where the local authority has systems to respond to incidents it becomes involved in a larger number. A major finding of the survey was the lack of clarity about roles and responsibilities. The preparedness of local authorities for incident response is linked to their understanding of roles and responsibilities. Local authorities have varying degrees of preparedness depending on the provision of skilled staff to respond to incidents 24 hours a day, availability of sampling, monitoring equipment and personal protective equipment, and financial resources for laboratory analysis and remediation (Fairman and Waterworth, 2001).

The regulatory framework for prevention of chemical incidents

A number of measures are in place to prevent the occurrence of chemical incidents:

- Land-use planning is probably the most important means of preventing potentially hazardous processes and plant being sited in residential areas. The Health and Safety Executive apply risk criteria in their advice to local authority planning departments that minimise the risks from new plants (HSE, 1989).

- A European programme exists for the risk assessment of all new and existing chemicals in the market (CEC, 1993a and 1993b). This should lead to controls being placed on chemical production, labelling, and use restrictions that prevent risks to health and the environment.

- The classification, packaging and labelling of chemicals is covered by health and safety legislation applying United Nations standards of protection (The Chemical Hazard Information and Packaging Regulations 1994).

- The transport of chemicals is subject to a number of internationally agreed controls. EC Directives are intended to ensure their proper enforcement. Controls exist on transport by sea, rail and road. Requirements on labelling and transport packaging exist (Carriage of Dangerous Goods (Classification, Packaging, and Labelling) Regulations 1996, Carriage of Goods By Rail Regulations 1996, and the Carriage of Dangerous Goods by Road Regulations 1996).

- Sites where specified quantities of specific chemicals are stored or handled must be notified by their operators to the Health and Safety Executive under the Notification of Installations Handling Hazardous Substances Regulations 1982.

- The approval, sale, supply, storage and use of pesticides is controlled by the Control of Pesticides Regulations 1986. These are enforced by the local authority where the pesticides are for domestic or home use and by the HSE where there is use at work.

- The safe use of chemicals, training of operatives, and implementation of controls and safe systems of work for the use of chemicals are controlled by the Control of Substances Hazardous to Health Regulations 1999.

- Certain high-risk industrial plants come under the Control of Major Accident Hazard Regulations 1999 that implement the Seveso II Directive (96/82) to prevent and limit the consequences of major accidents. Such sites must plan for accidents, implement controls and emergency procedures and provide information to local communities. The Directive and Regulations have led to an intensification of the involvement of local authorities in major hazards (Haigh, 2000). Emergency planning officers (EPOs) are now responsible for drawing up off-site emergency plans. The site operators must also enter into an agreement with the local authority as to how the public is to be informed of the correct behaviour in the event of an accident.

- All other activities are covered by occupational health and safety at work legislation. Although lower-risk plants and processes may not have to plan for accidents, risks posed need to be assessed and managed under the Management of Health and Safety at Work Regulations 1999.

- Various controls exist on specific polluting processes. Although these are aimed at limiting routine, not accidental, emissions, they aim to ensure good operation of plant and so help in the prevention of accidents. The general framework of control is through Integrated Pollution Control (IPC) but will be superseded over the period to 2007 by Integrated Pollution Prevention and Control (IPPC) that applies to a large range of industrial installations, and is aimed at preventing problems from routine emissions from plant. Specific controls on emissions exist such as those in the 'Solvents Directive'. This Directive aims to reduce routine emissions of volatile organic compounds from industrial installations.

All legislation is available free from www.legislation.hmso.gov.uk. Guidance documents are often available free on the appropriate government department's website (accessible through www.open.gov.uk).

Section Two

Preparedness

The preparedness phase – the period before an incident happens – involves setting up an efficient system for emergency response and remedial action influenced by experience from previous incidents or training sessions. During this phase decisions can be made by consensus. For environmental health practitioners preparedness will involve, first, being clear as to the nature of their own and others' responsibilities and, second, putting in place systems for responding to incidents. Chapters 2 to 4 outline roles and responsibilities in relation to chemical incidents. Chapters 5 to 12 raise issues relating to preparedness that local authorities need to consider.

2   The role of the local authority in chemical incidents

Local authorities provide a range of services at local level. This book focuses on the role of environmental health practitioners (EHPs) in incidents, but they need to act with other local authority staff and others for an effective intervention. The role of the local authority in chemical incidents will be broad, and should be defined by the local authority emergency plan.

Local authority services are provided by a number of independently operating departments and divisions of different professional groups. The services provided will be at either district or county council level, or through a unitary or metropolitan authority. Many departments have a role to play in managing chemical incidents, and many have information important in the overall response.

The **Planning Department** controls local development and land use. It may be important in prevention and preparedness as it is likely to have detailed information on the siting of hazardous installations and local developments. It may also have access to Geographical Information Systems (GIS) that are useful in incident preparedness.

The **Highways Department** will be important in any incident arising from road transportation of chemicals. It also has responsibility for any substances dumped or spilt on the public highway.

Social Services may play a role in the aftermath of a major incident with the provision of counselling. They will also be responsible for the provision of social work advice and assistance.

The **Housing Department** may play a role in providing temporary housing for those affected by an incident.

Building Control will give advice on structural safety in the event of building damage related to an uncontrolled release or explosion.

Environmental Health Services may have a regulatory role to play in controlling the incident. They also have a wider role in assessing the health hazard and ensuring, as part of a team, that the risk is managed in the interests of the health of the community.

Emergency Planning has a vital coordinating function. Emergency planning units are normally based in the county or unitary authorities. Their main role is to coordinate responses at emergency incidents through pre-incident planning. This is usually organised through a joint committee of representatives of the emergency services and local authorities.

In the event of an incident or emergency, the emergency services may request support services from a local authority. This is typically done through planning links established by the EPO, acting as a contact point for organisations in the area. Although local arrangements vary considerably in detail, in larger incidents, the EPO may well play a role in acting as a single point of contact for emergency services wanting access to local authority services and facilities. This might involve triggering the appropriate parts of their authority's emergency plans and, if the incident is large enough, acting as a link between the authority and the emergency service strategic command throughout the incident. See the case study in Box 3.

Box 3 Interdepartmental cooperation

A liquid petroleum gas cylinder exploded and was catapulted through the roof of an adjacent building and landed in a factory yard causing an oil tank to rupture. The environmental health service coordinated the response. Those involved included Building Control, Highways staff, the Environment Agency and the emergency services. The building had partly collapsed and needed demolition. The factory opposite had to be evacuated. The highway needed to be closed and the watercourse needed to be protected. EHPs liaised with and coordinated all parties, kept neighbouring authorities informed and dealt with the press. This incident is a good example of different departments of the same local authority working together to provide an effective resolution.

3 The role of environmental health practitioners in chemical incidents

In local authorities, the professionals charged with a 'health' remit are environmental health practitioners (EHPs). They are concerned with assessing, controlling and managing those aspects of the natural and built environment that affect human health. Factors affecting health are diverse and include biological hazards in food, chemical hazards at work and safety hazards in dwellings.

EHPs attempt to control these factors by using legislation and other methods such as education or persuasion. Much of the confusion over the role of EHPs in chemical incidents arises from the lack of a specific duty for local authorities to investigate and manage chemical incidents. This does not mean that EHPs have no role in chemical incidents. Far from it! Chemical incidents can only be successfully managed by joined-up working by a range of professionals with different skills:

- emergency services supported by the local authority to deal with the initial incident;
- primary medical services to deal with any casualties;
- environmental health staff to assess the extent of the exposure of local communities to the hazards and to effect a control;
- local/district health authority public health staff to assess the health implications of that exposure.

If any member of the team is not present or prepared, then managing the incident successfully may be difficult.

The role of the emergency services and primary medical services is clear. The public health medical role has been defined by guidance that places responsibility for the surveillance and handling of the health aspects of non-communicable environmental hazards on health authorities (DH, 1993). Health authorities are encouraged to have contracts with regional service provider units, of which there are five across the country.

The EHP function post-accident may be clear, but during an incident it can be imprecise. A number of publications refer to the role of environmental health services and the local authorities. The National Health Service (NHS) Guidance concerning Planning for Major Incidents identifies the essential elements to ensure an effective response to a major incident (DH, 1998) and states that in the event of a major incident the role of local authorities often includes the coordination of an emergency planning liaison group. It envisages that this role will be performed by EPOs and EHPs.

The Department of the Environment, Transport and the Regions (DETR) publication *Environmental Sampling after a Chemical Accident* provides guidance on the sampling procedures to gauge the nature and extent of contamination from a chemical incident (DETR, 1999). The report's intended users include EHPs. It suggests that EHPs may be ideally placed to play an initial investigative role following a chemical incident, be involved in a response team attending the site and carry out environmental sampling.

A Health and Safety/Local Authority Enforcement Liaison Committee (HELA) circular advises local authority enforcement officers on major incident response procedures (HELA, 2000). It advises that local authorities should be involved in the event of a major incident, and have emergency procedures and arrangements for dealing with one through their role in emergency planning.

There may not be a specific legislative duty to assist in chemical incident management, but it is very likely that the emergency plan refers specifically to environmental health involvement in incidents (for example see Lancashire CC, 2000; BESMIC and HESMIC, 1997).

Box 4 An emergency plan

To protect the health of the community by providing assessment of health risk and recommending and implementing remedial action in cases involving, for example:

- Hazardous emissions
- Toxic materials
- Communicable disease
- Contaminated food and water supplies
- Flooding and damage to goods and services
- Rabid animals
- Temporary mortuary provision.

(LB Southwark, 1999)

Box 4 gives an example of how a London Borough's emergency response plan defines the environmental health role.

The overall responsibilities of the local authority and the environmental health service are determined by local agreement, but a good example of an incident plan coordinated by a county council is given in Box 5.

Figure 1 Probable EHP involvement in chemical incidents

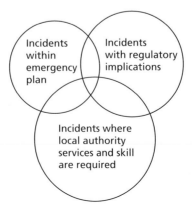

Box 5 Local authority reponsibilities defined by the emergency plan

Responsibilities of District Councils

General

To determine the risks to the population and the environment, and to take action in conjunction with the Emergency Services and other agencies to minimise the effects of the incident on people.

To ensure the safety of food and water supplies.

To assess any damage to the local environment including its contamination and to ensure that the public is not exposed to any associated risks.

To provide temporary emergency accommodation for people made homeless.

To effect a clean–up of all areas affected by the chemical incident.

To make the necessary arrangements for, and to ensure suitable disposal of, all affected materials to an approved disposal site.

Responsibilities of the Chief Environmental Health Officer

To provide initial advice on the environmental effects of the incident, pending more detailed investigation.

To carry out investigations and take samples to assess the effects of an incident.

To maintain close liaison with the Emergency Services, District Health Authority, public analyst and other agencies involved in the incident.

To ensure that the water supply remains wholesome and presents no risk to consumers.

To oversee environmental clean–up to ensure that the public is not exposed to contaminated residues.

To attend the incident control centre on request.

To make an initial assessment of the incident to determine if a Chemical Health Hazard (i.e. a chemical incident) exists, in consultation with the DHA's designated officer (CCDC) and hospital Accident and Emergency consultant.

(Lancashire County Council, 2000)

The EHPs' probable role in chemical incidents is shown in Figure 1. It shows three primary reasons for environmental health involvement – emergency planning, regulatory responsibilities and the general duty of care by the local authority.

Probably the most influential guidance on environmental health roles in chemical incidents comes from the Chartered Institute of Environmental Health in its guidance document *The Role of EHOs in Emergency Planning: Professional Guidance* (CIEH, 2000). While acknowledging that the role must be determined by the local authority itself, it advises:

As a general policy … and not least in the light of their new powers under the Local Government Act 2000, the CIEH considers that it would appropriate for Departments to take on the wider role in protecting the health of the local community and involve themselves in incident management.

Acceptance of such policy advice will mean that environmental health services will be involved in chemical incident management with the wide aims of protecting public health.

4 The role of other agencies

A multitude of agencies and organisations can be involved in chemical incidents. The actual involvement depends upon the nature and scale of the incident. This chapter details agencies' responsibilities and likely roles in larger incidents, but it is not exhaustive.

The Emergency Services

Police

The police are likely to be the first service alerted during a serious chemical incident. Their main responsibilities are control and coordination (apart from an area where a fire is taking place) to ensure the protection of life and property, including securing and making a site safe, although this function is frequently delegated to the fire service. The control functions relate in particular to the general public at the incident scene and in the surrounding area, including advising, warning or evacuating those who may be endangered (Irwin et al., 1999). The coordination functions involve liaison with the other emergency services, including provision of communications, maintaining access and egress, and assisting in dealing with casualties.

Fire service

The primary responsibility of the fire service is to deal with emergencies involving fire. In these situations they take charge. They will attend chemical incidents that do not involve fire, but they may not take charge in these circumstances as they have no statutory duty to become involved. Apart from protecting life and property, their role may include rescue, providing advice on dangers and evacuation in connection with dangerous substances, requesting local authority assistance, decontaminating and treating spillages.

The fire service use their own chemical databases, e.g. CIRUS or CHEMDATA, maintained by the London Fire Brigade and the National Chemical Emergency Centre (NCEC), which provide information on the chemicals and hazards involved, precautions and personal protection. Fire services have their own trained officers, hazardous materials officers, and specialist equipment including bulk foam units for flammable gases, and major incident units with additional breathing equipment.

Ambulance service

The ambulance service's primary role is to advise on and coordinate medical provision at the site of an emergency, attending to immediate medical needs and subsequently transporting any injured persons to their treatment centres.

The National Health Service

District level

The NHS Executive circular HSC 1998/197 has stated that health authorities in England and Wales must have adequate arrangements for dealing with chemical incidents and that there must be a designated individual responsible for ensuring that appropriate plans for the district are prepared. In the majority of cases this individual is the consultant in communicable disease control. Local links are important for inter-agency networking to local authorities.

Regional level

In the UK, Scotland, Wales and Northern Ireland each have one regional office and England has eight. The health emergency planning advisers are based in the region and are responsible for coordinating district level health authority plans. The advisers can provide inter-agency liaison and where appropriate, may be able to provide comment on local authority emergency plans for chemical incidents overall. The advisers are accountable to their regional directors of public health.

National level

Health emergency planning advisers receive policy guidance from the Emergency Planning Control Unit of the Department of Health. This Unit also provides a spectrum of policy guidance to others, including other divisions of the NHS, other government departments and the voluntary sector.

Enforcement agencies

The Environment Agency (EA)/Scottish Environmental Protection Agency (SEPA)

The EA has statutory responsibility in connection with the pollution of air, land and coastal waters, and routinely deals with chemical incidents.

The Health and Safety Executive (HSE)

The HSE is the enforcement body that deals with protecting employees and the public from work activities. Although the HSE does not see itself as an emergency service, and has limited capability to deal with issues that occur outside office hours, enforcement issues arising from work-related chemical incidents are an HSE function.

The Food Standards Agency (FSA)

The FSA becomes involved in chemical incidents where there is potential contamination of farming land, crops and livestock, or food supplies. EHPs will work alongside the FSA in cases of food contamination.

Ministry of Agriculture, Fisheries and Food/Scottish Executive Agriculture, Environment and Fisheries Department (MAFF)

MAFF has some responsibilities in relation to chemical incidents and may be involved in response.

The Drinking Water Inspectorate (DWI)

The DWI audits the water authorities monitoring programme to ensure that drinking water complies with chemical, biological and physical standards and is wholesome and fit. It has powers to investigate and initiate enforcement action.

Industry

The water authorities

Water authorities are responsible for the supply of drinking water and for the collection and treatment of wastewater. In a chemical incident the role of a water company is to ensure that drinking water is safe to drink and use. If water is not suitable for use, an alternative supply will be provided. In the event of surface or groundwater pollution the water authority will ensure that any drinking water abstraction points are not affected. Where chemicals have been disposed of to the foul sewer, the water and sewerage companies aim to prevent their discharge to the aquatic environment and prevent them from disrupting normal treatment processes.

Organisations providing advice

Regional service provider units/chemical incident response services

Health authorities should have a chemical incident advisory service. In the UK a number of providers of this service are in operation. In England, Wales and Northern Ireland health authorities should ensure that there is a contract with a provider. These providers are officially termed regional service provider units but are commonly called chemical incident provider units. The provider units also render services for local authorities.

Providers include:

- Chemical Incident Response Service, Medical Toxicology Unit, Guy's and St Thomas' Hospital NHS Trust, London covers the NHS regions of South East, South West, Eastern, Trent, London and the North West. Information about the CIRS can be found on http:// www.medtox.org.uk

- Chemical Hazard Management and Research Centre, Institute of Public Health and Epidemiology, University of Birmingham, covering the West Midlands Region

- Chemical Incident Management Support Unit, University of Wales Institute, Cardiff, covering Wales and Northern Ireland

- Chemical Incident Service at the Department of Environmental & Occupational Medicine and Epidemiology & Public Health, University of Newcastle, Newcastle upon Tyne covering the Northern and Yorkshire Health Region and

- Scottish Centre for Infection and Environmental Health covers Scotland.

Scottish Centre for Infection and Environmental Health

The Scottish Centre for Infection and Environmental Health serves the public health community in Scotland. Under the NHS, it delivers an advice and support service, surveillance, education and training, and undertakes research on environmental and infection issues, including chemical incidents.

National Focus for work on response to chemical incidents and surveillance of health effects from environmental chemicals

The National Focus started in January 1997 with a remit to support the NHS in its response to chemical incidents. This includes national surveillance of chemical incidents, promoting suitable training and undertaking general coordination in promoting a consistent NHS response and approach to chemical incidents. It also has a remit to alert the Department of Health and activate the Health Advisory Group on Chemical Contamination Incidents (HAGCCI). Information on the National Focus can be found on http:// www.natfocus.uwic.ac.uk.

Health Advisory Group on Chemical Contamination Incidents

The terms of reference of HAGCCI are to advise on request, urgently if necessary, any department of public health in the UK and the chief medical officers of the UK in the event of an incident leading to chemical contamination transmitted through environmental pathways (air, soil or water) which might affect health or cause public concern on health grounds, including:

- the extent to which illness occurring in the area following the incident may be attributable to the toxic properties of the contaminating chemicals;
- the likelihood of prolonged or delayed health effects;
- any diagnostic or therapeutic measures which should be offered to those affected, or to the whole population of the area;
- any epidemiological, clinical or other investigations required to determine the nature and extent of exposure of members of the public, body burdens or pollutants, and effects; and
- any long-term health surveillance required.

HAGCCI consists of an advisory panel of approximately sixty experts. Since being established in 1991, HAGCCI has been activated only once. While HAGCCI's remit is confined to larger-scale incidents with major public health implications, it needs information in order to brief ministers and respond to media enquiries. Since the introduction of the National Focus, responsibility for the activation of HAGCCI has passed to the National Focus.

CHEMSAFE

CHEMSAFE is the UK chemical industry response scheme to provide rapid expert advice and support to its members and the emergency services in the event of an accident in the transportation and distribution of chemicals. It can provide advice on hazards, skilled staff to attend the incident and appropriate specialist equipment.

The Environment Monitoring and Response Centre (EMARC)

EMARC is a forecasting service made available by the Meteorological Office. It provides storm tide forecasting, meteorological advice in the event of a marine pollution spillage and models the spread and concentration of atmospheric pollutants.

CHEMET (chemical meteorology)

CHEMET is a Meteorological Office scheme that provides advice to the Emergency Services in the event of a release of toxic chemicals, including plotting the plume dispersal. Another related role is that of PACRAM (procedures and communications in the event of a release of radioactive materials).

The National Radiological Protection Board (NRPB)

The NRPB has responsibilities for providing information and advice to persons (including government departments and health professionals) in relation to the protection of the community from radiological hazards. Advice is available on the hazards, environmental impact and risks to individuals that may arise as a consequence of an accident or incident involving ionising radiation. Many substances can be both radioactive and exhibit chemical toxic effects. The NRPB is also responsible for the coordination of the National Arrangements for Incidents involving Radioactivity (NAIR) scheme. This is a mechanism by which local police forces can seek assistance, advice and monitoring of radiation during an incident from competent authorities. The NAIR handbook is available from NRPB on request.

The Armed Forces

Due to their breadth of experience in dealing with crisis situations, and their training in nuclear, chemical and biological warfare, liaison with local military personnel to foster links may prove helpful to local authorities.

The Royal Mail

The Royal Mail can identify every property within any postcode and would be actively involved in the distribution of written emergency advice to the public, possibly as a special delivery.

5   Preparedness action at a local level

Once issues of roles and responsibilities are clear, preparing for chemical incidents requires planning in the following areas (IPCS, 1999):

- setting up a multidisciplinary response team and working arrangements;
- networking with interested parties;
- identifying the potential sources of chemical incidents in the locality (Hazard Profiling or Community Risk Assessments);
- conducting Baseline Health and if necessary Environmental Assessments;
- liaising with the local community;
- drawing up the chemical incident plan or covering issues in the emergency plan;
- establishing access to information sources; and
- pursuing measures to reduce the impact and likelihood of accidents at a local level.

A number of these preparedness issues are dealt with in the following chapters. Appendices contain more detailed information. Setting up a response team and networking is covered in Chapter 7 and hazard profiling and community risk assessment in Chapter 8. Chapter 9 covers emergency planning. Toxicology, standards and environmental sampling are dealt with in Chapters 10 to 12. Risk assessment issues are discussed in Chapter 13 and issues related to communicating with the public and the media are covered in Chapter 14 to 16. Chapter 17 deals with the important issue of liability.

Other issues such as pursuing measures to reduce the impact and likelihood of accidents are not specifically referred to in this section as they have been covered in Prevention (Section One) and Recovery (Section Four).

6   What happens during an incident

Incidents are rare and most environmental health practitioners will never be highly experienced in dealing with them. This chapter contains a brief description of what happens during an incident.

The management of the response is undertaken at one or more levels.

Operational (bronze) level management relates to the control of the site activities. For many incidents this will be the only level of control that needs to be established. Operational control will usually be conducted from a control point such as an incident vehicle at the scene. Possible tasks for environmental health at this command level are sampling, monitoring and risk assessment (Avon Health Authority, 2000).

Tactical (silver) level control will usually be established for more serious incidents operating from an incident control point in the vicinity of the disaster, but probably not at the scene itself. It allows tactical commanders to determine priorities and allocate resources. A tactical group will normally be established, which should include a public health physician and environmental health staff. The environmental/public health input in this group is to advise the tactical (silver) commander on the measures that are required to limit or prevent further exposure of the public to the chemical incident, and in the absence of a strategic (gold) level commander to advise about evacuation and sheltering. To do this they will have to conduct monitoring, sampling and risk assessments.

Strategic (gold) level control is rarely needed except for the largest incidents. If established, it will usually be at Police Headquarters. The purpose of this tier of management is to determine wider priorities and establish a framework within which tactical commanders may work. Many specialists will be involved at this level. The aim of the environmental/public health involvement will be coordination to ensure that cohesive advice is available on health, scientific and environmental issues. This will involve the development of monitoring and sampling strategies; evaluating the risks in light of the exposure data; results from sampling and epidemiological data; advising on health priorities; and advising on the necessary public statements about medical care, i.e. how to avoid exposure and probable effects of exposure (Avon Health Authority, 2000).

When an incident occurs, site employees or employees involved in the incident, and some or all of the emergency services attend the scene. If formal coordinating is required, an on-site operational command will be established. This is usually controlled by the fire brigade. If the incident becomes larger or there is a threat to life, property or public order, additional levels of command are initiated, usually with the police taking overall control of the management of the incident at the off-site tactical/strategic command centre. The strategic command centre should involve as many agencies as possible. Chemical incidents will pose health risks to those responding to them. These will be physical and toxic risks, and personal protective equipment needs to be worn. It will be necessary to control access to the site. The public, media and residents may try to gain access, thereby exposing themselves and others to risks. Casualties will be removed from the site, usually by fire brigade personnel through designated access control points. The casualties will need to be decontaminated when removed from the site, ideally in specialised decontamination units.

It is important for EHPs to report to those in command of the site, and never to attempt to gain access to areas of the site without specific permission from the command. Adequate personal protective equipment must be worn. EHPs will need some form of identification which the emergency services will recognise. A conventional authority card may not be sufficient, particularly if attendance at the scene has not been specifically requested or the emergency plan does not define the environmental health service role (CIEH, 2000).

7 The response team

Creation and membership

When a significant incident is identified, a local response team may need to be formed to investigate the toxic hazards and risks and to coordinate counter-measures. One of the functions of this team is to provide public and environmental health advice. Mechanisms for providing this advice vary throughout the country: it may be obtained directly from the response team or via a sub-group of it. Public health advice should be drawn up following consultation between key professional groups, including:

• public health consultants in communicable disease control/consultants in public health medicine
• directors of public health
• local authority EHPs
• county/unitary authority emergency planning officers
• ambulance service representatives
• fire service representatives
• police representatives
• press officers
• clerical support.

The group providing public health advice should be able to obtain further information from a variety of sources, including:

• accident and emergency consultants (provider unit)
• consultant physicians
• medical toxicologists from an RSPU/chemical incident provider unit
• health authority managers
• nursing officers
• regional epidemiologists/Scottish Centre for Infection and Environmental Health
• FSA
• MAFF
• EA/SEPA
• HSE
• water companies
• occupational health physicians
• legal advisers.

Terms of reference

Given the stress of responding to an acute incident, it is essential that public/environmental health advice is drawn up in a structured manner. Agreed terms of reference should be available before an incident. These should include consideration of the following issues:

- agreeing and assigning responsibilities
- stressing the confidentiality of information
- establishing an incident room in a health authority/local authority building (this may supplement the police local emergency centre)
- arrangements to coopt other members as appropriate
- reviewing the evidence to date – toxicological, epidemiological, environmental
- determining level of resources required – staff/financial
- agreeing requirements for media information
- identifying a single spokesperson for the team
- minuting meetings and agreeing actions
- monitoring progress
- agreeing that all decisions should pass through the committee
- agreeing on further investigations
- interviewing cases and collecting data
- evaluating exposure histories
- ownership of data
- producing a final report
- auditing the management of the incident
- making recommendations about future plans
- making recommendations about future training requirements for those involved in response
- agreeing authorship for any subsequent publications.

As each of the organisations is autonomous, they may not initially agree these items.

8 Hazard profiling, documentation and community risk assessments

In order to plan for chemical incidents, environmental health services and health authorities need to produce a profile of:

- the baseline health and other information in their area; and
- the potential sources of chemical incidents, e.g. all industrial and commercial sites using chemicals, transport networks, and contaminated land in their area.

Establishing communications with neighbouring local authorities and health authorities is important. Sources of information on chemical hazard sites may be outside the local authority. It is necessary to ensure that information is shared and distributed amongst the agencies involved in incident management.

Baseline Health Information

To measure the impact on health of a chemical incident release, it is necessary to know the background levels of illness in the community before the release. The purpose of a baseline survey is to set up systems and to check whether the levels are normal or indicate existing chemically related health effects (IPCS, 1999). The health authority will take the lead on the establishment of health data for the district's population. This will include:

General health statistics – these are normally collected on a wide geographical basis, which may make it difficult to identify any changes in the health of an affected population. Specific epidemiological studies can be conducted around potential accident sites but they are very expensive and usually impractical.

Sentinel health events – this is the occurrence of a preventable disease, disability or untimely death which serves as a warning signal that a hazardous environmental exposure may have occurred. A sentinel health event system uses the same datasets as the more general surveillance system but focuses on a limited number of priority diseases. The diseases can be monitored using death certificates or hospital discharge data.

Hazard profiling for the area and the development of community risk assessments

Information on hazards and potential sources of chemical incidents within an area needs to be collated. It is possible, using this information, to conduct an assessment of the severity of the potential effects of a chemical incident in the local area. This involves:

1. the identification of hazardous chemical sites and other commercial and industrial premises using significant quantities of chemicals, pipelines and transport routes;
2. the identification of vulnerable populations, facilities and environments;
3. the identification of possible incident scenarios and their exposure pathways; and

4. an estimation of the health impact of potential chemical accidents, and the requirements for health care (IPCS, 1999).

Hazard profiling and thereby developing a risk assessment is a multidisciplinary task involving local authority environmental health services, other enforcement agencies such as the Environment Agency and Health and Safety Executive, and the health authority.

1 The identification of sites using chemicals, pipelines and transport routes

Hazard profiling is a task that local authorities are ideally placed to undertake. Planning procedures often provide information as to the intended use of sites, and planning is one of the best methods of prevention of accidents. The environmental health service holds information on sources of potential contamination and accidents through its pollution prevention and control functions.

The Environment Agency for England and Wales has produced an online GIS system that highlights sites with major polluting potential, sites of special scientific interest and watercourses (www.environment-agency.gov.uk). It is very likely that local authorities will be aware of the major chemical sites in their area. The following are information sources, many held by the local authority, which will enable a hazard profile to be defined. Other sources of information within and outside the local authority that should be consulted in building up a hazard profile are:

- planning professionals
- emergency planning officers
- fire services
- Health and Safety Executive
- Environment Agency/Scottish Environmental Protection Agency.

Identifying hazardous sites

It is important to remember that chemical incidents can arise from the use of chemicals in a large range of premises. These include large COMAH sites, but also smaller industrial and commercial premises using chemicals such as swimming pools, premises under IPC/IPPC control and sites that are not currently under any legislative control.

Control of Major Accident Hazard (COMAH) sites

Industrial sites that pose major accident hazards must be notified to the Health and Safety Executive and Environment Agency/Scottish Environment Agency. Sites that come under the COMAH Regulations 1999 must prepare a major accident prevention policy. Top-tier sites with greatest potential for accidents must prepare safety cases, and operators of such sites must prepare internal emergency plans. Local authority emergency planning sections are heavily involved in top-tier sites because of their need to prepare off-site emergency plans, and will be aware of lower-tier sites, chemicals stored on-site, and the nature of the operation. Information on COMAH sites can be obtained from emergency planning units, the Health and Safety Executive and Environment Agency/Scottish Environment Agency. The COMAH Regulations replace the Control of Industrial Major Accident Hazard Regulations (CIMAH).

Non-COMAH sites

Authorised/permitted industrial process   Under Integrated Pollution Control (IPC) and Integrated Pollution Prevention and Control (IPPC), public registers are held by local authorities and the Environment Agency/Scottish Environmental Protection Agency. These list industrial sites and processes that have been authorised/permitted to release substances to air, water or land. At the moment the two control regimes are running in parallel. Both IPC and IPPC require the operators of polluting industries to apply for 'authorisations' or 'permits' to pollute. The information provided and the conditions of the authorisation/permit are held on publicly accessible registers. Local authorities hold public registers that contain processes and installations regulated by themselves and by the Environment Agency/Scottish Environment Agency. The Environment Agency/Scottish Environment Agency holds a public register of the polluting companies they regulate within IPC/IPPC. These registers provide valuable information on chemicals, their mode of use in a process or site and the controls in operation.

Nuclear installations   Identifying local nuclear installations should not be difficult. Nuclear sites are licensed by the Nuclear Inspectorate of the Health and Safety Executive under the Nuclear Installations Act 1965. This includes nuclear sites under the control of the Ministry of Defence, which comply with the same regulations. All sites are under the control of the Ionising Radiation Regulations 1999 and are required to have contingency plans to protect the public in the event of a release of radioactivity. These plans must be exercised as part of the licensing requirements.

Contaminated land sites   Local authorities are under a duty to identify contaminated land within their area under the Environmental Protection Act 1990 (as amended by the Environment Act 1995). They must develop a strategy to identify each site, assess the risks posed by the contamination on or near the site to the intended users and ensure that it is remediated by the polluter or owner. In identifying sites, they will use historical data, Ordnance survey maps and guides specific to industry sectors help identify pollutants associated with each industry. Public registers are held of sites where remediation notices have been served. In many local authorities more detailed registers were developed under s143 of the Environmental Protection Act 1990. Although the powers under this section were never bought into force, the registers hold much information that could be useful in hazard profiling.

Existing information sources on contaminated land include the derelict land survey (DoE, 1988) and a database of environmentally hazardous sites set up by Landmark Publications, a private company available online.

Identifying transport routes and hazards

International controls exist on the transport of dangerous goods and chemicals. However, the legislation does not allow local authorities to control routes through their areas on the basis of hazards. As the local authority will not be aware of the nature and amount of chemicals being transported through its district, it will have to assume that all major road and rail freight routes will carry hazardous materials and take a worst-case scenario approach. When chemicals are transported, there must be clear labelling information that assists in hazard profiling.

Figure 2 Vehicle hazard warning panels

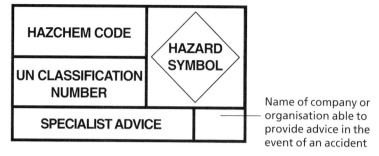

HAZCHEM CODE	HAZARD SYMBOL
UN CLASSIFICATION NUMBER	
SPECIALIST ADVICE	

Name of company or organisation able to provide advice in the event of an accident

Examples

© HMSO 1996

Source: Road Transport Carriage of Dangerous Goods (by Road) Regulations 1996

HAZCHEM is a UK statutory scheme for marking vehicles carrying bulk quantities, i.e. more than 3000 litres (see Figure 2). UN classification numbers are placed next to the HAZCHEM placard on the body of the tanker.

The HAZCHEM code gives information under the following headings;

* fire-fighting

* personal protection – the level of protective clothing to be worn

* risk of violent reaction

* spillage

* evacuation.

The code consists of one digit and one or two letters e.g. 3WE. The digit refers to the fire-fighting methods to be used. The first letter (P, R, S, T, W, X, Y, Z) refers to the spillage action to be taken. A second letter E is added for public safety advice. Although evacuation may be necessary, it may be safer for individuals to remain in a building rather then evacuate. Copies of the HAZCHEM code are carried by the emergency services.

The UN classification number is an individually agreed four-digit code for a specific group of chemicals, e.g. 1789 indicates hydrochloric acid and NOS signifies Not Otherwise Specified.

A contact number for specialist advice in case of emergency is included in the panel. CHEMSAFE is an advice scheme for the emergency services and a network of member companies able to attend incidents has been established. Members of CHEMSAFE also undertake to supply the National Chemical Emergency Centre (NCEC) with copies of safety data sheets. NCEC is staffed 24 hours a day and can provide information and advice should a chemical company be unidentifiable or unavailable. The Chemical Emergency Agency Service (Chemaid) is provided on a commercial basis with charges based upon the number of products transported. Companies provide the NCEC with details of products in an agreed format, and are then allowed to display an NCEC telephone on their vehicle hazard warning panels or packaging labels. The emergency services can obtain the necessary specialist advice for any products by contacting the centre directly.

'Tremcards' are normally carried in the vehicle and provide written instructions to the driver of the action required in the event of a spill or fire. Most of the cards in the UK are prepared by the European Chemical Industry Council using a system of standardised phrases and are available in 18 languages.

Material safety data sheets contain information on the hazards of the chemical, spillage and remediation advice.

Identifying pipelines

Emergency planning units will have details of pipelines carrying hazardous substances. Extensive pipeline systems are used to transport chemicals in installations such as oil refineries. Gas and oil is transported by pipeline. The transport of hazardous chemicals in pipelines is controlled by regulations. Local authority planners may also have extensive information on pipelines via the planning process.

2 The identification of vulnerable populations, facilities and environments

It is important to determine the nature of the natural and built environment in an area and of the local community, under the following headings.

Population

Establish the age and gender profile of the district's population and which are the major population centres. Identify any vulnerable populations such as schoolchildren, those in hospital, residential homes for the elderly etc.

Socio-economic description

Identify the economic basis of the district – industrial, agricultural or mixed.

Geography

This includes:

- watercourses within the district – sources and run-off. Water authorities should be able to advise if any watercourses are used for domestic water provision;
- low-lying areas or valleys where a toxic plume may persist for a prolonged period;
- location of new, current and disused industrial installations and their relationship to population centres, health care facilities, schools, leisure centres and transport. Access to up-to-date maps of the district is vital;
- location of recreational centres, local authority evacuation and reception centres, stockpiles of blankets and other resources needed during a major incident.

3 The identification of possible incident scenarios and their exposure pathways

For each site identified, it will be necessary to identify chemicals present (current and planned) and to develop for each of them possible scenarios of release. It may be possible to map the exposure pathways for each site and substance. This depends on knowledge of

- local topography from maps and other sources such as planning departments;
- local geology, which will be essential for the contaminated land strategy;
- watercourses and aquifers (contact the Environment Agency); and
- prevailing weather features.

4 Assessing the possible health impact

The populations within the exposure pathways that could be affected are then identified, with an emphasis on any especially vulnerable group e.g. children, the elderly, or those in hospital. Facilities that may be disabled in the event of an accident should be identified, as should important ecological sites. Assessing the vulnerability around transport routes will present greater difficulties, but consideration should be given to road, rail and inland waterways. The evidence from the exposure and vulnerability stages should be bought together to anticipate and estimate the likely impact in terms of health of both severity and numbers of injuries. This should be conducted either by the health authority or in conjunction with them, as it will be vital in informing them of health care requirements.

The hazard profiling/community risk assessment will assist the local authority in

- preparing a chemical incident plan or defining their role in the emergency plan;
- identifying equipment required for sampling and monitoring;
- identifying training needs within local authority staff; and
- ensuring the provision of a service that is capable of responding to likely accident scenarios.

Tools

Geographical Information Systems (GIS)

GIS are useful in that they are computerised mapping systems on which all hazards, populations, sensitive ecological areas and vulnerable populations can be plotted. Plume rise and water run-off modelling can be used with GIS and the impact of chemical incidents can be identified on a geographical basis. Many local authority planning departments use GIS, as do emergency planning departments. Some local authority environmental health services use GIS to plot information relating to contaminated land, sites authorised/permitted under IPC/IPPC, COMAH sites and information on the types of premises within their areas.

Fate and transport of pollutant models

Few local authorities are likely to have a full range of fate and transport models. However, the national air quality strategy and local air quality management have meant that many authorities have purchased or have access to air dispersion models. Such models can be used to track the likely dispersal of a plume from an acute incident.

Risk assessment models

Many formal risk assessment models exist. Brief information sources on risk assessment can be found in Appendix 12. More detail on software, databases, consultants, directories etc. can be found in the European Environment Agency publication, *Environmental Risk Assessment: Approaches, Experiences and Information Sources* (Fairman et al., 1998).

9   The local authority emergency plan

In the context of chemical incidents, the most likely calls on EHPs might be for advice on the nature of hazards and potential effects both to people and to the environment, requests for monitoring services, and advice/assistance with post-incident clean-up.

The planning required to ensure that the environmental health service is prepared and able to respond to these demands needs to be documented as part either of the local authority emergency plan, a departmental generic emergency plan or a specific chemical incident management plan. The production of a departmental generic emergency plan may be preferable, as there may be significant chemical incidents that do not trigger the activation of the local authority emergency plan. Specific chemical incident plans, although recommended by IPCS, may be difficult to keep updated and relevant.

Most departmental plans will be 'generic', covering a range of situations and levels of involvement. They are usually support documents rather than sets of instructions, and place significant reliance on the underlying professional competence of responders. There is a trade-off between the degree of detail given and the inherent flexibility of the plan to cope with previously unidentified situations.

It cannot be emphasised too strongly that plans must be produced with full participation from all stakeholders. Plans produced *for* departments, rather than *by* them, are unlikely to be anything more than paper exercises, as people are unlikely to identify with them, or be familiar with the contents. For this reason, it is not appropriate to produce a 'model' plan that can be adapted for individual departmental use. Plans should not assume that individuals will be prepared to respond, or will undertake particular tasks, unless this has been confirmed with them and any necessary training given. This applies equally to plans produced by other organisations, for example site-specific 'major hazard' plans which might assume an environmental health input.

The term 'the plan' covers agreed arrangements and procedures, as well as the physical document. The 'procedural' aspect includes:

- the agreed roles and responsibilities of the department and of individuals, together with any 'Memoranda of Understanding' establishing or setting limits to them;
- relevant standing orders such as mutual aid arrangements with other authorities and associated liability indemnities, and authority to incur expenditure;
- agreed standby and 'on-call' arrangements;
- arrangements to validate and maintain the plan itself;
- documentation procedures to demonstrate that staff have been correctly trained, and are competent to undertake any monitoring and advisory role they may be called upon to perform. In chemical incidents, proof that health and safety training has been adequate may be particularly important.

Practical measures covered may include:

- procedures to be adopted to manage any incident, such as the composition and responsibilities of response teams;
- procedures to maintain 'business as usual' in the remainder of the district, such as reallocation of duties to free response team members;
- any agreements which have been reached to 'cascade' information to others, such as the Health and Safety Executive local authority unit or other specialist sections within the National Health Service;
- staff welfare and support arrangements;
- arrangements for plan activation and out-of-hours call-out;
- arrangements for maintenance of and access to protective equipment, stocks of sampling equipment etc.;

Additional contents would usually include:

- resource location/contact reference lists, staff telephone numbers, contact numbers for other agencies, emergency services, district health authority staff, key-holders, contractors etc.
- a checklist, or *aide-mémoire* of the measures individuals must take.

Administrative contents might include:

- serial number, and a page for noting amendments and updates, to 'track' individual copies so that no one applies obsolete procedures.

This might result in a fairly bulky document. Many of the contents listed above are needed to establish that the plan has been correctly set up, verified and maintained, but may not be needed during the management of an incident.

In an emergency, all that responding staff may want is a quick reference guide, and the simpler it can be made, the better. The essential parts are the resource/contact lists in some convenient format and the checklist/*aide-mémoire* section. If space is included for actions to be signed off when completed, this might form part of an incident action log which, as a 'contemporaneous document' may be useful in subsequent inquiries.

Simply supplying staff with the plan document itself is not sufficient.
Plan validation procedures must ensure that everyone is fully conversant with any role they may have to perform. This includes their 'normal' role and any others they may be called upon to perform, such as deputising for others who may not be available.

Remember that if an incident results in an inquiry or litigation the plan itself may have to be produced for examination.

10 Toxicology

Toxicology, the science of poisons, defines the internal and external factors which determine and modify the harmful actions of chemical substances, investigates the biological effects of chemicals and assesses health risks. In their role of protecting environmental health, environmental health practitioners (EHPs) use exposure standards that are based upon toxicology. EHPs should understand some of the basic toxicological mechanisms in order to assess exposure and apply standards properly. It is not expected that EHPs will necessarily be making toxicological judgements, but they need to have enough awareness to recognise when specialist advice is required.

Under different temperature and pressure conditions, chemical substances change from one physical state to another. The risks associated with differences in physical form depend upon the exposure context. For example, an ingot of lead could cause physical injury if dropped, but if heated and vaporised might cause serious systemic toxicity. Respiratory system damage may be caused by materials in various physical states – solids, liquids, gases, vapours, fumes, mists and aerosols – and systemic absorption will distribute such substances widely throughout the body.

Dose and response

The dose–response relationship is a useful indicator of the toxicity of a chemical. The most toxic substances, such as botulinum toxin, need to be present in body tissue in only trace amounts (less than 5 ng/kg) to exhibit a toxic effect or to prove lethal to humans. For some chemicals, such as pharmacological drugs, dose and response are well understood. For industrial and environmental chemicals, there may be a paucity of data.

Toxicokinetics and toxicodynamics

Toxicokinetics is the study of the time course of absorption, distribution, biotransformation and excretion of compounds. Toxicodynamics is the study of the effects of compounds upon the body. These studies assist in evaluating concentrations of toxic chemicals in biological samples such as blood and urine from people exposed to chemicals.

A summary of the routes of exposure, absorption, distribution and excretion of toxic substances throughout the human body is given in Figure 3. Details of absorption, distribution, metabolism and elimination are not given here, as they are available in textbooks listed in the References. Remember that individuals exposed to chemicals may absorb them through more than one route. For instance, a gas cloud may lead to inhalation, ingestion, dermal and ocular exposure.

Figure 3 Summary of routes of exposure, absorption, distribution and excretion of toxic chemicals in humans

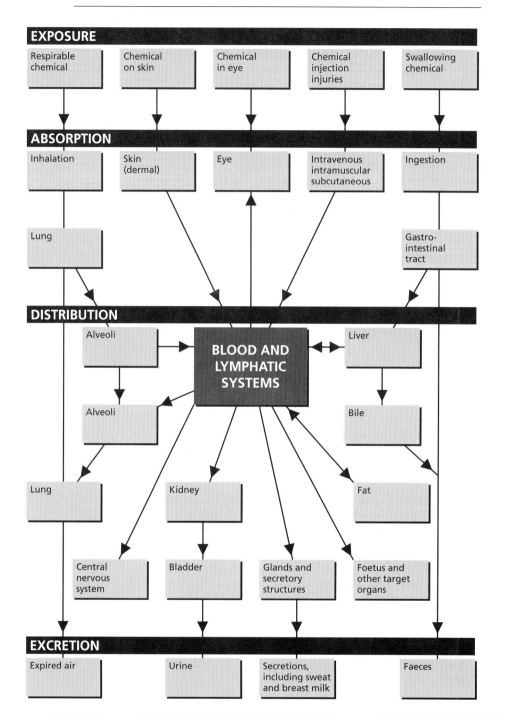

Source: V. Murray (1986) 'Assessment of the Risk of Exposure', in Ward Gardner (ed.) *Substances Hazardous to Health*, Kingston upon Thames; Croner Publications.

Individual susceptibility

The response of individuals to toxic substances can differ. An individual's age, sex, current health, nutritional and hormonal state can all influence their susceptibility to exposure to a particular toxic chemical. Concurrent exposure to other chemicals and individual genetic variations may affect susceptibility.

To assess the toxic hazard to an individual requires assessment of

- factors that may affect susceptibility
- exposure levels
- exposure routes and the likelihood of absorption
- whether the absorption will result in a toxic effect, and
- whether the effect will be immediate or delayed.

Classification of toxic effects

Toxic effects can be classified based upon

- *Chemical classification* – this is useful in predicting effects from single substances or groups of similar chemical substances, e.g. heavy metal poisoning or polyaromatic hydrocarbon poisoning.

- *Temporal classification* – this reflects the response over time to chemical exposure and the resultant toxic effect. Definitions of acute and chronic effects are inevitably arbitrary, but the following are suggested:

  - Acute effects occur immediately or within 48 hours of exposure, e.g. asphyxia from cyanide or euphoria, hallucinations and coma from inhalation of trichloroethane.

  - Chronic effects occur after a latent period between exposure and outcome, sometimes many years later, e.g. mesothelioma and lung cancer from asbestos or peripheral neuropathy from solvent inhalation or exposure to some pesticides.

- *Clinical classification* – this encompasses clinical effects produced by chemicals, e.g. allergenic respiratory effects due to formaldehyde; irritant effects – eyes, skin, mucous membranes due to chlorine; carcinogenic effects – angiosarcoma of the liver and vinyl chloride.

- *Pathological classification* – this is concerned with medical toxicological effects including those identified by target organ toxicity, e.g. central nervous system – anaesthetic and narcotic effects from hydrocarbons; peripheral nervous system – peripheral neuropathy due to lead; cardiovascular system – myocardial infarction among viscose rayon workers exposed to carbon disulphide; renal and hepatic damage – carbon tetrachloride and some anaesthetics.

When interviewing potential victims to assess the nature and degree of exposure, identify the symptoms, and encourage them to seek medical advice if any appear.

11 Exposure standards – What they mean and how to interpret them

Standards defining 'how much' of a chemical an individual can be exposed to exist for a number of substances in different exposure scenarios. Although it is tempting to employ them because of their apparent simplicity and their use in other areas of environmental health, **exposure standards should be used in emergency situations with extreme care**. This is because they:

- are developed for a specific exposure scenario, e.g. occupational and environmental standards differ not only because of the time period of exposure but because of the population they cover and the social factors which affect what is acceptable in each scenario.
- are often time-weighted. Environmental sampling results may not be.
- often relate to a potential lifetime exposure and may be inappropriate to use in an acute exposure setting.
- are often based on feasibility and practicality rather than health, e.g. some occupational exposure levels and water standards.

If in any doubt as to the appropriateness of the environmental standards in use, or when actual exposure is very close to the exposure standard, expert toxicological advice should be sought. This is available from the RSPU/chemical incident provider units through the local health authority.

Land exposure standards

Standards for contaminants within land will be set according to the legal control regime in the Environmental Protection Act 1990 (as amended by the Environment Act 1995). They will be produced by the Contaminated Land Exposure Assessment (CLEA) model and will define the acceptable concentration of a contaminant per unit of soil and relate to a specific land use. At present the only guidelines (relating to land contamination) are those set by the Interdepartmental Committee on the Redevelopment of Contaminated Land (ICRCL) and Dutch soil criteria. These guidelines have no regulatory status.

Water exposure standards

Drinking water standards exist for contaminants in water. These are specified as contaminant concentration per litre of drinking water and are based upon a lifetime's exposure to the contaminant. They are European Union standards and are normally enforced by the Drinking Water Inspectorate (DWI) which audits the monitoring results carried out by water authorities. EHPs will become involved where water in local authority premises is supplied from local authority tanks or private water supplies. Health-based WHO guidelines exist for drinking water.

Air exposure standards

Air standards differ from those for land and water in that they are time-weighted. This is because the concentration of chemicals in the air varies substantially, both over time (temporal variation), and over space (spatial variation). Some chemicals may have an acute or chronic effect. Air standards must therefore take account of the spatial and temporal variations in contaminant concentrations and the chemical's mode of effect. Standards relate to specific defined periods of exposure.

Using air standards can therefore be problematic. Concentrations of toxic chemicals within a plume from a fire are only present for a short time and are affected by environmental and weather conditions. Specialised equipment is often needed for representative air sampling taking account of the spatial and temporal variations. Monitoring needs to be carried out quickly due to the transient nature of the plume. In spite of these difficulties, inhalation of contaminated air is likely to be the route of exposure that causes most concern for health during or in the immediate aftermath of an incident.

UK Air Quality Standards (AQS) apply to air and are environmental exposure standards. They should be applied to emergency incidents with care. The statistical basis of some standards means that they are difficult to apply. Some are based upon rolling means; others are based on long exposure times. There are only eight AQS at present.

The WHO has set air quality guidelines for a larger number of contaminants. Again they may relate to time periods of exposure not useful in an emergency or its aftermath.

These environmentally based air standards exist for a limited number of chemicals. However, there are about 500 Occupational Exposure Limits (OELs). These are standards for societally 'acceptable' concentrations of chemicals in air to which workers are exposed. They do not relate to environmental exposure. However, OELs are often the only standards that exist. Various rules of thumb are used to convert these standards (which are based upon an 8-hour exposure during a working day for a whole working life) to standards that can be applied to environmental exposure. Generally the Occupational Exposure Standard/40 is used as a rough guide for environmental exposure (Hall and Kukadia, 1993). For those particularly hazardous or difficult-to-control substances that have been set a Maximum Exposure Limit (MEL), the MEL/100 is a guide for environmental exposure. HSE documentation on OELs is useful for providing background information in assessing the potential impact of the hazard. Information about the types of hazards posed by the chemical, the way the chemical acts in the environment, e.g. half-life and information on safety precautions can be gained from safety data sheets supplied by manufacturers or criteria document summaries produced by the HSE.

Emergency standards have been set by the American Industrial Hygiene Association (IPCS, 1999). These standards have not been tested in the field and their use cannot be recommended.

Appendix 8 contains information sources related to standards.

When using standards, the following should be borne in mind:

• The standard used will determine the nature of the environmental sampling. The time frame the standard is based on will determine the time frame required for sampling, e.g. OELs are time-weighted averages so that results from grab sampling are difficult to use.

• What are the main absorption routes? If people are exposed to chemicals that can be absorbed through the skin, such as organic solvents, and the skin is a likely exposure route, reference to an occupational exposure standard is not helpful. This is because the OEL is based upon inhalation as the exposure route.

In the next chapter environmental sampling will be discussed in the light of these issues.

12 Environmental sampling

To be able to assess the potential health impact of an incident on the local population, the toxicological information needs to be combined with information on the doses of chemical that people have received. Exposure standards normally relate to an environmental concentration of a chemical. These environmental concentrations are based upon the dose of toxic substance they give rise to when absorbed and metabolised by the human body.

Environmental health practitioners are primarily concerned with human health impacts. Sampling may need to be conducted in order to

- enable assessments to be made on the immediate health impact;
- enable decisions to be made on sheltering and evacuation;
- determine the remediation required; and
- provide information for follow-up epidemiological inquiries and surveillance.

Sampling during an incident may be difficult and should not be attempted without consultation with the emergency services. If conducted, consideration must be given to the safety of the person carrying out the sampling, and adequate personal protective equipment (PPE) worn and safety procedures followed. Appendix 2 defines PPE needs.

Sampling Strategies

To approach sampling in a cohesive and planned manner, the EHP should design a monitoring and sampling strategy, based upon the aims of the sampling and the proposed uses of the data, the degree of accuracy required, the speed of response required, the likely contaminants, the important exposure routes, and the resources available. The aim of the strategy is to ensure that samples are representative of the environment from which they are taken.

What is the aim of the sampling?

If the aim is to determine the presence of a chemical, a relatively simple method can be used. Air can be grab- or spot-sampled using grab sampling or Draeger or colorimetric tubes. Soil, water and deposits can be sampled in an *ad hoc* manner, by selecting contaminated media. Samples should be taken at different times and in different locations so that they are representative.

If the aim is to compare the samples with exposure standards, they should be over the same time period as the standard, or should be readily convertible to that period.

How accurate do you need to be?

Obviously sampling should give accurate, representative results. In an emergency with limited time, a more pragmatic approach may be needed. It may be necessary to obtain instantaneous data. Unless expensive continuous monitoring equipment is available, visual observation or basic sampling equipment such as detector tubes may be the only option. If the concentrations of contaminant causing an effect are very small, such as with highly toxic pollutants, accuracy may be highly important. If legal proceedings are possible, demonstrably accurate results are necessary.

How fast is a response required?

During the incident, information is normally required as quickly as possible. It may be that only *ad hoc* or visual observations can be made. With chronic contamination or when immediate acute effects are not likely, a more detailed sampling strategy will be possible.

Which samples to collect?

The types of samples needed during or directly after an incident depend upon the possible routes by which the public are exposed to the chemicals.

Different types of incident have the potential to affect different media; this is depicted in Table 1.

Table 1 Media affected by release

Type of release	Affecting the following media	Resulting in the following exposure routes in order of importance
Release to air	Air, land and water by deposition	Inhalation, ingestion of soil, crops, livestock, water secondarily contaminated, and from consumer goods
Release to water	Water, land, air (through volatilisation, aerosols, splashes etc.)	Ingestion of water, ingestion of soil or contaminated crops and livestock, inhalation, e.g. cooking, showering
Release to land	Soil, watercourses, air (if volatile), secondary contamination of crops, drinking water	Ingestion of soil (children), ingestion of contaminated crops, livestock or water, inhalation, e.g. dust

What type of chemical is likely to be present?

If the EHP does not know the chemical involved, the operator of the industrial process should do. The fire brigade may have information. If chemical packaging exists, labelling information should have hazard markings. The chemical incident provider units may be able to assist in identification. The likely constituents of fires are given in Appendix 7.

Where to collect them?

Initial sampling required during or shortly after the incident needs to focus on

- areas with the greatest contamination; and/or
- areas with the highest population densities or the most sensitive populations, e.g. schools or hospitals.

This is a 'worst-case' approach. Predicting the geographical areas where contaminants may be heaviest is either based upon professional judgement (e.g. when predicting where oil from a tank may leak, the slope of the ground, the soil type and the topography need to be considered), or on modelling (e.g. the grounding of a plume from a fire can be estimated by plume modelling). Further details can be found in Appendices 5 and 6.

If results are not required immediately, the aim of the sampling strategy will be to produce samples representative of the environment. This will mean not concentrating on worst-case contamination.

What resources are available?

A major issue for EHPs will be the availability of sampling equipment. This may be fundamental in determining the sampling strategy.

Producing a sampling strategy helps to ensure the appropriate use of resources, that samples are suitable for their intended use and that they best represent the level of contamination posed by the chemical incident. The following section will concentrate on sampling equipment. This is an important preparedness issue.

Sampling equipment

It is recognised that not all local authorities are equipped with sophisticated sampling equipment. As part of the preparedness strategy information should be collected on where such equipment can be obtained or details of specialist organisations that provide sampling services.

Water, soil and deposit samples

Water, soil and deposit samples are relatively easy to take with limited resources. The equipment comprises sealable receptacles in which samples can be transported to the laboratory. Attention needs to be paid to the nature of the chemical being sampled, and the material of the sampling receptacle. For example, volatile hydrocarbons will permeate a polythene bag.

Appendix 2 highlights equipment requirements. Appendix 3 outlines some of the issues to be considered in sampling, including protocols. Although water and soil are easy to sample, analysis may be expensive.

Air samples

Air samples providing meaningful results are difficult to take. Equipment is expensive and not widely available. Ideally the exposure data gained should be over a reasonable time span, which may be difficult in an emergency. The data should give details of changes in concentrations over time and space. For this information very complex monitoring equipment is required, capable of continuous real-time analysis. For most local authorities such equipment is not available and other resources must be investigated. Where such equipment is available, it may provide useful data on air quality.

Detector/Draeger tubes

These provide an instantaneous reading that indicates contaminant concentration. They are not precise. The results can be interfered with by similar chemicals to the one measured. They measure only a 'spot concentration' and cannot be said to be representative of the incident site. They do not measure a time-weighted average and the results are difficult to compare with exposure standards. However, they are cheap, easy to use and widely available, and in many incidents may be the only sampling equipment accessible. Results should be treated with caution but may be useful if verification that a chemical is present is all that is required.

Active sampling

Sampling equipment used in occupational air sampling is often available to local authorities. Air is drawn through a filter for a known period of time. The filter can be analysed at a laboratory and a time-weighted average obtained. High-volume samplers can be 100% efficient for fine particulate matter. Specially modified high-volume samplers will be required when sampling the products of a fire. This involves a filter to remove the particulate and an adsorbent to remove the volatile fraction. Because of the time delay caused by laboratory analysis, active sampling may be more useful in assessing environmental exposure in the non-acute stage of an incident.

Grab samples

For purely gaseous releases a grab sample can be collected in a container. The choice of container depends upon the reactivity of the gas. Normally bags are constructed of polyester film, PVC film or Teflon or Teldar, and are filled by pumps with inert interior surfaces or by indirect pumping.

Using national networks to provide a sample

If an accident occurs close to an air quality monitoring site, it may be possible to analyse its filters for contaminants of interest captured from the release. If the contaminant of interest is one that is monitored, then real-time data can be obtained from www.aeat.co.uk/netcen/airqual/.

Real-time sampling

Mobile real-time sampling equipment such as Mobile Infra Red Analysers (MIRAN) and Photo Ionisation Detectors (PID) will provide the most accurate and useful information. It is not widely available. Some local authorities own such equipment and lease it to other authorities. Such arrangements need to be organised so that 24-hour availability of equipment is possible. This requires planning but the advantages are obvious.

Current guidance

The DETR publication *Environmental Sampling after a Chemical Accident* is a comprehensive guide to sampling procedures and protocols and provides EHPs with practical advice (DETR, 1999). It is not directed at sampling to assess human health impact but is useful in laying down sampling protocols. The publication is aimed at EHPs and provides advice on best practice, but has no legal status. One potential shortcoming with the document is that the primary exposure route EHPs will deal with is inhalation of contaminated air and the document pays little attention to this issue.

13 Risk assessment

Risk assessment attempts to give an estimate of the extent of harm that may arise from an incident. It does this by examining the manner in which the local community has been exposed to chemicals released, and by relating the potential doses they have received to health effects. Risk assessment should be a joint exercise between the environmental health service and the health authority. Because of the nature of chemical incidents, the immediate initial assessment should be based upon a worst-case scenario approach, especially when data are missing or are of dubious quality. Caution must be exercised in the use of such approaches for fear of causing distress or alarm. It is very likely that when urgent management decisions are required, either during or in the immediate aftermath of an incident, a risk assessment based upon qualitative data will be the only type of assessment possible. As more time and resources become available the assessments will tend to be based upon more quantitative data. Whatever the nature of the data, the risk assessment process is the same. Risk assessment requires two vital components:

• Data on exposure of the local community and therefore on doses

• Data on toxicological properties of those chemicals at those doses.

Qualitative risk assessment

There are a number of steps in risk assessment. These are discussed elsewhere (IEH, 1999; DETR, 2000; Fairman et al., 1998). In chemical incidents a risk assessment will:

1 Formulate the problem

It is vital that all parties involved in the incident agree on the nature and extent of the assessment. This is necessary because the way the problem is formulated in the minds of the incident team will determine their actions. For instance, is human health hazard alone or wider environmental hazard being assessed? Are possible interactions of the chemicals released with existing contamination to be looked at? These issues need to be defined at an early stage so that sampling, monitoring and resources are targeted in an efficient and effective manner.

2 Identify the hazards

Identify the chemical/chemicals released and use information sources, health authorities and their RSPU/chemical incident provider units to determine the nature of the hazards. Do they present chronic or acute effects? What time scale of exposure is required for effects to take place? The safety data sheets or other sources of relevant basic information on hazards, remediation etc. should be obtained. Appendix 4 contains sources of information on chemicals.

3 Determine who is exposed, and by how much

In the initial stages of an incident, when difficult decisions need to be made on evaluation, sheltering and public information, very limited exposure data will probably be available. A precautionary approach needs to be adopted in the face of data gaps. *Any monitoring data at this stage is better than none.* If an identifiable link can be made between those exposed and the source, it will be necessary to gauge how much contaminant is likely to have reached the local population. The degree of exposure will depend upon

- how much chemical was released, e.g. if small quantities of chemical are released into very windy, stormy conditions, the exposure of local communities is likely to be small;
- the exposure route, e.g. contaminated water is a much easier route to control for human exposure than contaminated air;
- how close the local population are to the release and the topography in between, e.g. is the local community based in a valley with a chemical spill above them; how close are they?
- the weather conditions, e.g. is it raining, what is the wind direction and speed?

If quantifiable data are available, then decision-making will be easier. If not, a judgement needs to be made about the likely exposure of the local population in the light of the above factors. Any sensitive populations need to be identified and special consideration given to the elderly, the young and those in hospital. It is possible to describe the activities of the local population in relation to the contaminant either by observation or by using activity questionnaires. This assist assessments of how often and to what degree the population may have been exposed to the contaminant. Questionnaires should be drawn up in association with the health authority.

4 Estimate the effect of that exposure

This is primarily a public health function, but EHPs should consider the degree of toxicity of the chemical and its absorption routes in their judgement of the likely exposure. It may be that a chemical is only absorbed efficiently through the lungs, but the emission is to water. Therefore, unless vaporisation is an issue, the risk will be low.

5 Determine what remediation measures are required

There are likely to be a number of ways that the effects of the chemical incident can be mitigated and controlled. These will include actions to address the immediate acute impact of the incident and longer-term actions if chronic effects are likely. Management options can include decisions such as whether to let a fire burn or to put it out, whether to use a chemical dispersant in an oil spill and whether to evacuate people or recommend sheltering. The function of the environmental health input, together with that of the public health physicians, is to advise the emergency services of the implications of their actions and the best option for the health of the public.

Risk assessment by quantitative measures

A quantitative risk assessment is possible if there are

- good exposure data describing the doses of contaminant that the local community have been exposed to. This will be obtained from either environmental monitoring, biological monitoring (e.g. looking for biomarkers in blood, urine or faeces), or modelling the fate and transport of the contaminant in the environment and exposure;

- good data on toxicity of the contaminants released by the incident. There is a general paucity of toxicity data, and major difficulties in relating the data often obtained from occupational exposure to other exposure scenarios.

Obtaining such data is difficult and means that quantitative risk assessment is expensive, time-consuming and resource-intensive. In certain situations, however, it may be necessary (Fairman, 2000). These include:

- where there are controversial issues with a high degree of media attention;
- where remediation measures are very expensive and/or disputed;
- where the public are very anxious about possible chronic health effects.

Quantitative risk assessment is a multidisciplinary task requiring the skills of the health authority and local authority EHPs. External environmental consultants may be required if fate and transport modelling, extensive environmental sampling or exposure modelling is required.

The health authority is likely already to be conducting health impact assessments which describe the nature and severity of the health effects that *already exist* in the local community (see BMA, 1998 and IPCS, 1999 for a description of health impact assessments). The results of the quantitative risk assessment will be a description of the *likely effects and impacts* (many of which will not have been reported or have manifested themselves) of the incident on the health of the local population. This will include the number of people likely to be affected, the nature and severity of effect, the numbers of sensitive people affected, the geographical distribution of the people affected etc. The health impact assessment and the quantitative risk assessment together will enable options for management and remediation to be established.

The benefits of a quantified risk assessment approach include:

- analysis of the existing and potential impact of the accident;
- identification through exposure route analysis of the most critical exposure pathways and routes of entry;
- identification of particularly sensitive groups or geographically most exposed areas and communities;
- the possibility of analysis of the impact of various remediation options on the distribution and nature of health effects;
- the justification of costs of remediation in terms of reduction of health impact; and
- the justification of actions resulting from the risk assessment in terms of their rationality.

The difficulties of a quantified risk assessment approach include:

- cost in time and resources;
- the specialised nature of the task may mean that skills are not available and consultants have to be used;
- the highly scientific nature of the assessments can often exclude the local community from the process so that the assessment may not be trusted, especially if there is suspicion about the source of the assessment or data used;

- the exclusion of issues such as emotion, psycho-social factors and values. This can be seen as positive from a rational viewpoint, but often rationality is not the factor that guides decision-making. Exclusion of these factors means that the assessment is not trusted.

Information sources on risk assessment can be found in Appendix 12.

14 Public safety – sheltering versus evacuation

Background

In a chemical incident where the public may be exposed to a toxic vapour cloud and the risk of fire and explosion, two options for protective action exist – sheltering or evacuation.

At present EHPs may only rarely be involved in the decision-making process. The decision on what, if any, action should be taken in an acute incident usually rests with the police with advice from the fire, ambulance, health and social services. As part of a developing integrated approach to all incidents, the EHP and public health staff should be members of any response team. This means that emergency services, ambulance control and A&E departments will be more likely to involve them.

To participate actively, the environmental health service may need to contact the police to request that its nominated representative be included amongst those notified during an incident. If the EHP is called upon to give an opinion from the public health population-based perspective, familiarity with the issues involved will be useful. Any pre-existing local guidance/information should be obtained, in advance, from any COMAH site or nuclear installation off-site plan.

COMAH sites

COMAH site operators must supply safety information to members of the public resident in a zone liable to be affected by a major accident. The size of the zone concerned is established between HSE and the operators, and is typically an area within a 2 – 3-kilometre radius of the site.

Local households are supplied with information outlining the site activity, a description of the hazardous substances stored, a description of the emergency warning signal, e.g. activation of a siren, with details of siren tests and emergency action to take, e.g. effective sheltering, tuning in to radio frequencies for further instructions, etc.

The public near a COMAH site needs to be issued with these instructions for immediate action. There will probably be little time to give out information during the early stages of an incident. Even with low windspeeds of 2 m/s, the front of a gas cloud may have travelled 1.2 kilometres in 10 minutes, giving the emergency services insufficient time for pre-emptive action. The emergency planning officer will have a copy of this advice, which may prove helpful during an incident.

Radiological incidents

The need for evacuation in the event of the release or threatened release of radioactive material is addressed in *Arrangements for Responding to Nuclear Emergencies* (HSE, 1994). Advice should be sought from experts at the Health and Safety Executive and the National Radiological Protection Board.

Other information sources

Geographical Information Systems (GIS) may assist in mapping the potential spread of a toxic plume. The police and the fire brigade can consult CHEMET during an incident. An assessment of local weather conditions is made, and a fax is sent showing the probable drift of a plume. A qualitative risk assessment is required to assess the likely impact on residents of any potential exposure. Informed risk management decisions can then be made.

Sheltering or evacuation – the pros and cons

Sheltering – GO IN, STAY IN, TUNE IN

A considerable degree of protection is afforded by sheltering in a house. Buildings dampen fluctuations in atmospheric turbulence, reducing infiltration by gases. Even in a poorly sealed house infiltration may be reduced by a factor of 10. When windows and doors are sealed with wet towels or newspapers the factor increases to $30-50$.

Effective sheltering entails:

- closing doors and windows;
- minimising draughts by sealing windows and doors with paper/tape or damp towels;
- turning off central heating;
- turning off mechanical ventilation;
- going to an upper floor, if possible to an interior room where ventilation is less;
- avoiding bathrooms and kitchens, which tend to have higher ventilation rates;
- keeping pets indoors;
- breathing through a wet cloth over the face if the atmosphere becomes uncomfortable;
- having access to a radio to tune into the local radio station for further information and advice.

The public need to be advised not to use the telephone unless vital, to prevent unnecessary jamming of lines. They may be asked to notify neighbours who may not have heard the warning.

Communication systems must be in place to ensure that people go outside into the fresh air as soon as the hazard has passed. If inhabitants remain sheltered for too long they could be exposed to a higher cumulative dose than they would have received outside. Some people may be severely incapacitated and will need to be assisted from their homes.

Evacuation

Evacuation is a measure of last resort when the public would be in serious danger if they stayed. Specific instances would be:

- **Before an incident (precautionary)**
  - Risk of imminent explosion
  - Small leak likely to escalate sharply
  - Release/threatened release of radioactive materials.

- **During an incident**
  - Spread of fire or continuation of a hazardous release over a prolonged period
  - Continuing release of a hazard over a prolonged period of time.
- **After an incident**
  - Gross or persistent environmental contamination.

The decision to evacuate to minimise the risk to public health should always be taken in conjunction with the health authority.

Evacuation is feasible only if it can be confidently predicted that there is sufficient time to evacuate people before the incident escalates.

The time available to effect evacuation will depend on:

- the time required to make the decision to evacuate – the emergency services' response time;
- the time required to communicate with the public – depending on method chosen, e.g. door to door, via loudhailers, radio/TV networks, any language barriers, whether translators are needed;
- the time of day – it is more difficult to warn people effectively at 4 a.m. than at 8 p.m.;
- the time necessary for the public to prepare to move – to collect clothes, medication, baby supplies, pets, cheque books, credit cards, and to secure their homes;
- the time required for the public to move.

Evacuation of homes may not be appropriate in a short-term release of potentially toxic gas, e.g. chlorine.

The decision to evacuate is also affected by:

- the population profile – numbers of elderly, disabled and immobile, whether there are any residential/nursing homes in the area, the number of people with special needs living in institutions, any people on dialysis machines or others at special risk;
- the extent of the road network;
- transport availability – public and private (in the UK, 30% of households do not have a car and will need assistance);
- blockage of roadways, e.g. flooding, snow;
- hazardous travel conditions, e.g. fog, sleet, ice, snow;
- the health risk to the police cordon;
- consideration of the effect on evacuees of outside temperature, psychological trauma/medical risks, risk of damage and looting to property and cost;
- how large a zone should be evacuated.

Checklists for assisting in evacuation or sheltering decision-making and in deciding whether it is safe to return to homes after evacuation are included in Appendix 13.

15 Risk communication

Communicating about risks to public health can be a difficult task. The Department of Health has produced some *Pointers to Good Practice* that give an overview of the complexities of risk communication and lay down a framework for good communication (Department of Health, 1999). For EHPs, risk communication is part of their everyday work. In spite of this, successful communication of difficult risk issues requires clear organisational objectives, planning, policy and training.

In communicating risk EHPs need to look at issues much wider than the preparation of messages and the release of announcements, although these are important. The public reaction to risk often seems bizarre, especially when compared with scientific estimates. It is important for EHPs to understand why public reaction to risk can differ so much from what the evidence would suggest. Until recently the prevailing view has been that the public are simply irrational when worried unnecessarily about low-level health risks. There is now widespread acceptance that the reaction of the public to risk is not irrational but based upon issues that relate to

- the characteristics of the risk;
- the trust they feel for the people and organisations giving them the risk message;
- the degree of media sensitisation to the risk; and
- the extent to which they are involved in two-way communication.

Trust is easily lost. Building it is a long-term cumulative process. Short of a reputation for infallibility, the single most important factor is openness. This involves not only making information available but giving a candid account of the underlying evidence (Department of Health, 1999). Certain types of risk are known to have characteristics that alarm the public. These include situations when the risk is involuntary, when it inequitably distributed and so on. It appears that these characteristics reflect fundamental values and cannot be dismissed as irrational. Because of the factors that affect risk perception, the use of risk comparisons should be avoided. Comparing the public health risks of one issue with another familiar accepted risk (such as crossing the road) may appear to put the risk into perspective, but is likely to backfire, especially if involuntary and voluntary risks are juxtaposed. The framing of the risk message is important. Risk has different meanings for different people, and incorporates different issues. The understanding of probability and very small numbers varies a great deal among the public. The way messages are framed needs to take account of this diversity. However, it should not be assumed that the public will not understand complex information. Uncertainties should not be covered up, as research indicates that this reduces public trust.

Box 6 Fright factors

A risk is more worrying (and less acceptable) if it is perceived

1 to arise from a man made, novel source,

2 to be inescapable by taking personal precautions,

3 that its effects are irreversible and hidden,

4 that small children or pregnant women are at threat and

5 that it is poorly understood by science.

Adapted from Department of Health (1999)

When dealing with chemical incidents, crisis conditions can often militate against effective communication. However, with the 'Fright factors' (Box 6) and the 'Media triggers' (Box 7 in the next chapter) in mind, consideration can be given to planning and preparation for risk communication. It is important that the organisation behaves in a manner compatible with the message. If the message is 'Don't panic', desperate and uncoordinated action by the organisation will undermine the message, e.g. giving the public information that a plume from a fire is non-toxic at the same time as ordering sheltering or evacuation.

The Department of Health publication on risk communication is valuable reading for all EHPs whether dealing with incidents or not. For a good summary of the pros and cons of different methods of communicating risk, see SNIFFER (1999).

16 Communication during a major incident

One of the most critical factors in responding to a major chemical incident is communication. No single agency in the UK has overall responsibility for coordinating this aspect of the response. It is essential that all agencies involved in incident response liaise with each other and participate in joint exercises regularly, to ensure that any communication problems are identified and remedied.

Good communication will also help to ensure that each organisation is informed of an incident at an early stage. If this notification comes from a number of allied agencies, so much the better. Each agency should draw up procedures for communicating within the organisation and with other agencies, the public and the media.

The general public will need information and advice, particularly those affected by the consequences of the incident. Cooperation and openness with the news media will alleviate some of the inevitable pressures that occur, help restrict the spread of rumours and present a professional image to the world.

Within the organisation

The need for rapid communication between local authority personnel, both outside and inside the local authority headquarters, means that an incident room, with a number of computer and telephone points which can receive direct dialled calls, is likely to be necessary. Telephone numbers should be kept secure for emergency use only. Arrangements whereby emergency services can request that non-essential users are temporarily disconnected must be considered: many local authorities will not be identified by the emergency services as essential users. Similar arrangements exist for British Telecom terrestrial lines and will require further investigation by the emergency planning officer.

With allied agencies

Regular routine contact with allied agencies will help improve communication and may allow alternative communication methods to be used during an incident. Systems should enable the establishment of rapid and secure communication links with allied agencies, including health service professionals.

With the public

Handling the press is an integral part of incident management. The public appetite for information should not be underestimated. Parker and Baldwin (1994) describe public warnings during an emergency. They note that in an emergency, communication via local radio and television only reaches 51% of the population. Means of reaching the elderly and those living alone have to be sought.

It is vital to start providing information as soon as possible. One of the best ways of reducing worry and distress is to provide the public with adequate and credible information in a structured way. Parker and Baldwin suggest that warnings to the public must be given swiftly. They suggest three warning periods, starting when the population is first put at risk (not when the incident is discovered): 0–2 hours,

2–12 hours and 12–24 hours. The warning method depends upon the warning period.

First Period (0–2 hours)

Initially word of mouth is the only means available. This will involve as many agencies as possible. The initiating agency will declare a major emergency and inform the three primary support agencies – police, health and media. Statutory authorities and other agencies have a network of contacts that can be used to disseminate information from the centre.

Second Period (2–12 hours)

The media will still be involved in issuing up-to-date information. All agencies will be receiving phone calls from the public. All agencies must have the same briefing sheet to ensure consistent information.

During this period leaflets will be prepared and distributed to the affected population. As many as possible of the agencies already identified should agree the contents of the leaflet. The primary language of the target population should be considered. Distribution of the leaflets or pre-printed picture leaflets or cards should be coordinated by a central authority, nominated at the time, to ensure that there are no gaps in the content of the leaflet or its distribution.

Third period (12–24 hours)

During this period each household and commercial establishment should receive a written communication giving details of the event, the action to be taken by the population and the action being taken by the statutory authorities to ensure a return to normality.

Once an area has been identified by postcodes, the Post Office can identify every property in the area and deliver the letters.

End of incident

A further written communication should be delivered to the affected population.

Help line

During an incident it may be necessary for the lead health authority to institute a public help line. Arrangements for deciding when and how to institute a help line should be in place in advance (Stark et al., 1994). A room will need to be identified and arrangements be in place for staff to be seconded to work on the help line. Consideration should be given to the information that will be available over the help line, and the means provided to enable staff to identify and answer commonly asked questions. Systems for passing non-standard or difficult callers to senior staff should be developed.

Alternatively, NHS Direct is likely to be able to respond to and document many of the inquiries if provided with adequate information and support.

With the media

If the flow of information to the media is poor and the press subsequently report that they cannot establish details, the public may think that not enough is being done, that the local authority is not coping or that there is a cover-up. There are

Box 7 Media triggers

A possible risk to public health is more likely to become a major story if the following are prominent or can readily be made to become so:

1 Questions of blame

2 Alleged secrets and attempted cover-up

3 'Human interest' through identifiable heroes, villains, dupes (as well as victims)

4 Links with existing high profile issues or personalities

5 Conflict

6 Signal value: the story as a portent of further ills (What next?)

7 Many people exposed to the risk, even at low levels (It could be you!)

8 Strong visual impact (e.g. pictures of suffering)

9 Links to sex and/or crime.

Source: Department of Health (1999)

certain known factors that will increase the interest of the media in a chemical incident (see Box 7).

Dealing with the media should normally be through the public relations or press office. A single press spokesman who will provide the majority of the media information should be identified at an early stage (Dalkin, 1994). This individual may require a member of the environmental health services to speak directly to the media. A member of staff prepared to do this should be identified in advance. This should be someone with authority, a strong persuasive personality, and the ability to present information to the press with conviction. Close liaison with the public relations/press office is essential.

A number of smaller-scale incidents will attract considerably lower levels of media attention. A public relations officer should still ensure that the arrangements are in place for a consistent and coordinated level of response to be provided by all agencies, enabling their expertise and resources to be combined successfully with those of the local press, radio and television (BESMIC and HESMIC, 1997).

If the event is very newsworthy, the press will not only want daily press conferences but exclusives. Press access may require firm control. A consistent approach by all agencies is vital, and press attention should not be permitted to inhibit the work of the incident team.

When speaking to the media:

- Come to an interview with two or three key points you want to present to the public. If necessary, repeat them several times during the interview. Each key point should take the form of a 15–30-second 'sound bite' suitable for direct use.

- Assume the interviewer and the target audience have no background knowledge.

- Avoid jargon. Stories must be easy to listen to or read. If you present a simple message it is less likely to be edited and thereby distorted.

- Avoid gimmicks. They may lead to media exposure, but the gimmick is likely to be remembered, rather than the message.
- Always have a press release prepared which sets out the facts, e.g. the number of people exposed, the extent of exposure, any reported illness, the nature of remedial works being carried out and the public health message.
- Stay within the limits of your expertise.
- Be prepared for questions that you would prefer not to answer. Tell the truth but avoid speculation.

Technical aspects

A number of issues relating to the technical aspects of communication links need to be considered and resolved before an incident occurs:

- Ensure that agencies involved are identified as essential telephone users by the emergency services.
- Identify rooms with multiple computer and telephone points, and establish how easily these can be assigned direct-dial numbers.
- Determine the location of a help line, the choice of a telephone number for it and how readily available that number will be.
- Maintain an up-to-date contact list of out-of-hours contact details for the emergency services, local hospitals, local health authority, your RSPU/chemical incident provider unit and other enforcement agencies such as EA, HSE and FSA.

17   Liability

Environmental health services will be aware of the concept of a 'duty of care'. Some of these obligations are imposed by statute, e.g. the duty of care of an employer to protect the health, safety and welfare of his employees. Failure to honour them may result in criminal prosecution. Much of the work of EHPs is to ensure that others fulfil their statutory obligations.

In chemical incident management, particularly if EHPs have been acting in an advisory role, individual officers and the local authority as a whole must not be negligent. In legal terms an EHP or a local authority would be negligent if

- they owed the claimant a duty of care;
- they breached that duty of care;
- the breach of that duty of care resulted in loss or damage.

Establishing a duty of care

A duty of care may be established in a number of ways. The most obvious is where a statutory duty has been established under a specific piece of legislation. Failure to comply with specific legislation may be criminal in itself, but may also be used in a civil case to demonstrate that a duty of care exists and has been breached. Local authorities are themselves subject to such legislation, and may find themselves charged with negligence if they fail to provide statutory services in reasonably foreseeable situations. In emergency management the keeping of records of how the emergency was dealt with, and logging of decisions and actions taken and the reasons for taking them are essential.

In most routine situations the primary involvement of an environmental health service will be as an enforcement agency, ensuring that other organisations or companies (third parties) comply with legislation. Clearly, the third party has a duty of care to comply with statutory requirements, but there may also be a duty of care on both the service and the inspecting officer to carry out the enforcement role in an effective and competent manner. Increasingly where emergencies and accidents have resulted in compensation claims, both third-party organisations and enforcement agencies have found their activities subject to intense scrutiny for potential liability (CIEH, 2000).

A duty of care may also arise if it is accepted voluntarily. This may be regarded as a quasi-contractual obligation rather than a tortious one, but the effect is the same. If a department proposes to undertake a particular role in its emergency plan, then it has an obligation to do so carefully. Similar obligations exist if it agrees to a particular role or duty being incorporated into the planning arrangements of another organisation, or does not object if it becomes aware that such a role is proposed. The fact that this would be a voluntary rather than a statutory duty would be no defence. Once accepted, the duty must be performed.

Fulfilling the duty of care

In order to perform their duty of care local authorities must:

- ensure that they are clear as to their role in incidents;
- review how their emergency or chemical incident plans define their roles;
- ensure that staff are trained and competent to carry out the role;
- ensure that systems, procedures and equipment are suitable for the task.

Section Three

Response

The response stage begins once an incident has been recognised and lasts as long as rapid interventions are conducted. It is characterised by pressure of time, rapid decision-making, preferably according to a pre-arranged chain of command, and emergency responders' attempts to comply with an emergency plan or chemical incident management plan. The role of the environmental health practitioner (EHP) during this phase is to undertake risk assessments, collect data to determine exposure in the local population, provide the emergency team with local information and help determine management action. The EHP will also be vital in liaison between other services in the local authority and other enforcement agencies.

18 Managing an incident – some general considerations

Major chemical incidents can impose extraordinary pressures and demands on EHPs. As these incidents occur only rarely, few EHPs have gained sufficient experience for an automatic response. This section provides a basic approach to the environmental health response to a chemical incident. No two incidents are identical and all local authorities differ in their service provision. This section provides a framework for EHPs to develop local procedures and protocols. Local procedure should augment rather than replace the existing tried and tested local emergency plan.

Team approach

An individual cannot provide an adequate response to a major chemical incident. It is important to obtain help at an early stage. This may include rescheduling other routine duties, strengthening the on–call rota, securing adequate secretarial and information technology support, and dealing with domestic arrangements. Usually people are willing to help and need only to be asked. Colleagues tend to prefer involvement from the beginning of an incident. Their sense of ownership towards the response to the incident will be greater if they have been called upon early rather than as a last resort when events are threatening to overwhelm resources. Ideally all those involved in responding to an incident should be freed from other duties until it is clear that resources are sufficient.

A cohesive, multidisciplinary response to significant events such as major chemical incidents can be difficult to sustain. Individuals in the response team may not have had the opportunity to work with each other before, and may not fully understand each others' roles within the team or its aims. General and personal criticism by the press may disturb professional colleagues sufficiently to weaken the unity of the response. Confidentiality and trust must exist to minimise the chances that the group breaks down under pressure.

Record-keeping

Full and accurate records of events as an incident develops are vital. For the group, detailed minutes ratified at the start of each meeting followed by an incident report will suffice. As an aid to communication, it is useful to keep a list of all those involved, with their job titles, organisations and contact numbers accessible at all times. Those who attend meetings should be easily identifiable by secretarial staff, as teams may include a large number of unfamiliar individuals.

A detailed contemporaneous personal record of events should also be created. This will aid decision-making and serve as a record of personal roles in the incident, especially in the light of later inquiries. Personal records can also be used to assess the environmental health team's role, identify where improvements can be made and disseminate information to colleagues and students.

Assessment and decision-making

An acute incident requires an immediate response and assessment followed by a decision on whether to take action. An incident with a longer-term evolution requires immediate response and assessment, but less immediate action may be appropriate. Few incidents develop into major events. Frequent assessments should be made to review the severity and likely impact on human health and to determine when no further action is necessary.

19 Investigating the incident

EHPs need to provide a quick and effective response to chemical incidents. Most practitioners will have little specific experience of this, and they will have to rely on training and general professional knowledge. For an effective response, planning is necessary. In this chapter, a practical approach to responding to chemical incidents is outlined. Checklists and further information are available in the Appendices. The approach is not prescriptive but enables the production of local specific policy, planning and training.

From an environmental health viewpoint the objectives of the investigation are to

- identify possible regulatory implications;
- assess the acute impact of the incident and identify appropriate management approaches;
- assess the chronic impact of the incident and identify appropriate management approaches; and
- identify the cause of the incident with a view to securing appropriate control arrangements and prevent recurrence.

This chapter focuses on the initial response to an incident. During and in the immediate aftermath of an incident information and data are often sparse and decisions are required quickly. The assessment of chronic health risks will require a much more detailed analysis. Health impact studies will be conducted by the health authority and are described in many publications (see especially Irwin et al., 1999; BMA, 1998 and IPCS, 1999). Extensive environmental sampling may be necessary, possibly using environmental consultants. Quantitative risk assessment and health impact assessment cannot be covered in detail in this publication but information sources are listed in Appendix 12.

Using a tiered approach

To ensure the efficient use of resources a tiered approach to response is necessary. EHPs carry out many tasks, resources are often stretched, and the availability of staff out of hours may be restricted. The response of the authority needs to be tailored to the nature of the incident. Incidents posing major health risks must be dealt with immediately, with all available resources. Lesser incidents have lower resource implications.

The availability of out-of-hours staff is a particular problem. In a recent survey 66% of local environmental health services had a member of staff available 24 hours a day (Waterworth and Fairman, 2000). Although staff may be available out of normal hours they may not be experienced or qualified in the area of chemical incidents. Although many local authorities have EHPs available for 24 hours a day for noise nuisance investigation, the EHP may not have the necessary skills to investigate a chemical incident. A tiered approach, where an initial assessment enables less skilled staff to carry out the initial investigation and decide where further resources and skills are required, is useful in such cases.

Tiered approaches are also useful for an appropriate and proportionate response, and efficient use of resources. Figure 4 represents a tiered response in flow–chart form.

Figure 4 Tiered response actions

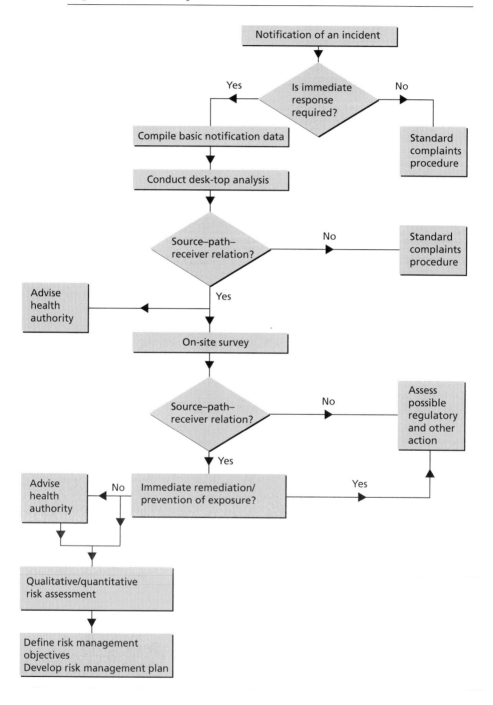

Desk-top study – the initial assessment

The purpose of the initial assessment is to determine whether members of the public are being exposed to chemicals and put at risk. The assessment of whether a 'source–path–receptor' linkage exists will determine future action.

A pro-forma checklist to be used during the initial investigation is found in Appendix 9.

The following information should be recorded:

• The date and time the event was notified, plus your own name and job title.
• The informant's name, position, job title, address and contact numbers.
• The nature of the site or type of business, and its full postal address including postcode.
• The name and telephone number of the on-site or off-site representative of the organisation.
• A brief description of the event:
  – What is known to have happened?
  – When did it occur?
  – What chemicals are thought to have been released?
  – What is the scale of the release?
  – What are the immediate problems?
  – What problems may follow?
• Who else has been notified or is in attendance?

Detailed information on the source and type of incident should be obtained as soon as possible. This may prove difficult, but should not delay assessment of those at risk and preventive safety advice where necessary.

In addition to the notifier the following may be useful sources of information:

• Premises files may give further contact details, and details of processes and operations.
• GIS or Ordnance Survey maps will provide maps for site or location plans.
• Public registers, i.e. Contaminated Land, Hazardous Substances, Public Water Supplies, Waste Transport and Storage Sites, Part B Prescribed Processes and A2 Installations.
• The Environment Agency GIS system on the Internet.
• RSPU/chemical incident provider units.
• Other Internet sources. Appendix 12 contains a list of websites, which may contain useful information.

Possible outcomes of the desk-top study are as follows:

• There is a possible linkage between the source of contamination and the public. A site visit will be required to obtain more information. Other agencies and organisations likely to be involved, possibly including the health authority, must be contacted.
• The incident is not an emergency as there is no possible exposure of the general public and it can be dealt with by standard procedures.
• No action is required by environmental health.

Site visits

The aims of the site visit are to verify the likelihood of contamination affecting humans, and to collect and document information about the site and the incident. Environmental samples can be collected during the initial site visit. The appropriate sampling equipment should be taken. Appendix 2 lists sampling equipment and personal protective equipment (PPE). Appendix 3 lists the issues to consider in sampling.

Safety issues

Site visits can only be made if the necessary precautions to protect the EHP have been taken:

- Obtain details of a designated safe approach route if applicable and avoid passing through any contaminants.
- Position your vehicle upwind of an incident and at a safe distance. Consider the multiple possible pathways for contaminants, e.g. through sewers and watercourses.
- If the emergency services are in attendance, report to the site controller on arrival and obtain permission to enter the incident area and advise.
- The appropriate personal protective equipment (PPE) should be worn at all times on site. Appendix 2 contains details of PPE.

The information from the site visit should include that outlined in Table 2. Appendix 10 contains a pro forma for collection of information based upon a risk assessment approach.

Table 2 Information needs and possible sources

Information required	Sources of information
What has happened and how did it happen?	Knowledge held by emergency services, other agencies (HSE, EA, health authority)
	Statements from witnesses
	Visual observation on site including damage, any identification information for chemical etc.
What chemical has been released?	Information from the management of the site or process
How much chemical has been/is being released?	Documentation from local authority files and public registers about chemicals stored or used or from EA
Is the release continuing?	Information from investigations by the emergency services and other agencies
	Information from witnesses
When will it stop?	Visual observation on colour and odour etc. of contaminant or plume, the nature and extent of the damage, and any evidence from packaging and labelling information. See DETR (1999). Appendix 4 details information sources on chemical hazards
	Environmental sampling. To enable analysis of samples the laboratory needs to know what substances to look for
	For likely contaminants in fire plumes see Appendix 7
Is any population exposed to the contaminants?	Use Ordnance Survey or GIS information to locate possible populations and identify exposure pathways, e.g. watercourses, sewers, land run-off, contaminated fire plumes etc.
	Visual observations on the extent of the contamination.
	Track the fire plume. The fire service has access to CHEMET for plume tracking. Some emergency planning units have plume prediction on local GIS. Some environmental health services have in-house air modelling capacity
	Evaluate whether a linkage exists between the source and the population potentially exposed
What are the meteorological conditions?	Visual observations
Are these likely to change?	Fire service has access to the Met Office
What likely concentrations of the contaminant is the local population exposed to?	Visual observations
	Odour threshold may be useful
	Conclusions from evidence of the amount of chemical leaked/ released and the transport of the chemical through the environment
	Environmental samples of the media most likely to be affected. Water and soil may be simple to take. Air is more difficult. See Chapter 12. Sample in areas of worst contamination or most sensitive populations. Appendices 5 and 6 provide information to determine extent of contamination and 'worst exposed' areas
	Exposure models based on activity questionnaires or reasonable estimations on the local population's activities in relation to the contaminant
Have any health effects been reported from exposed population?	Information from emergency services, health authority, witnesses

Note: If the emergency services are in attendance, the fire service should have obtained much of the information required for an assessment. They may have identified the chemicals, determined what safety precautions are necessary and taken steps to mitigate the effects of spillages and leaks of contaminants.

In addition to the above information, a description of the site, photographs and witness details should be taken.

Risk assessment

Chapter 13 sets out the overall process.

With the information provided by the notifier, other organisations and the site visit it should be possible to

1 Formulate the problem in association with others managing the incident

- What release and chemicals are being considered?
- Whom are they affecting?
- What mixtures of chemicals?

2 Identify the hazards

- What is the name of the chemical(s)?
- What hazards are associated?
- What remedial action is required?
- How much chemical was released and for how long?

3 Identify who is exposed and how much

- What is the size and nature of the population exposed?
- What is the fate and transport of the chemical(s) through the environment?
- What are the likely exposure routes for the population?
- What are the likely concentrations of chemical(s) in the environment?
- What are the likely levels of chemical exposure?
- Remember – *any monitoring data at this stage are better than none*, and if quantifiable data are available, decision-making will be easier.

4 Identify the effect of exposure

- The effect of that dose on the population is primarily a health authority function.
- Use standards, toxicology.

5 Identify the remediation measures required

- Define each containment option.
- Assess the impact on each part of linkage between source and receptor to determine the option with the best overall impact.

The International Programme on Chemical Safety has produced a simple schema to assist in achieving this (see Table 3). For each option it is necessary to describe the

- hazard
- exposure pathway
- route of entry

- actual/likely dose
- actual/likely effect.

Table 3 Best outcome assessment schema to plot the outcome of various options

Description of containment option		Hazard	Exposure pathway	Route of entry	Actual/ likely exposure dose	Actual/ likely effect, e.g. severity, numbers	Assessment of risk
No 1	Population						
	Environment						
No 2	Population						
	Environment						
No 3	Population						
	Environment						

Source: International Programme on Chemical Safety (1999).

Section Four

Recovery

The recovery phase lasts as long as the effects of the incident can be expected to persist. Generally, more time is available to make decisions than in the response phase. However, public and political pressure may place time constraints on the remediation action. Legal action could be involved and questions of recovery of costs during an incident may be important. Once the response phase is over, victims start the process of coping with the repercussions of the incident, and communities and the media tend to return to their usual activities and lose interest in the incident and its consequences.

20 Management of remediation and compliance with legislative standards

As time goes on and the emphasis switches to recovery, the local authority will take a leading role to facilitate the rehabilitation of the community and the restoration of the environment. (Home Office, 1997)

In chemical incident management, environmental health services have most experience of the management of remediation and compliance with legislative standards. This chapter will focus on the legislative provisions that may be useful in the remediation of chemical incidents, and some of the issues to be considered by environmental health practitioners (EHPs).

Areas that may require remediation measures will be identified from the risk assessment carried out during the response. In the event of chronic contamination, qualitative or quantitative risk assessment should identify the areas of risk and the most appropriate remediation. Examples of possible areas requiring attention are:

- deposit of fibres, e.g. asbestos
- deposit of combustion products
- contaminated land
- contaminated watercourses
- contaminated water supplies
- contaminated drains, culverts and sewers
- contaminated buildings and ventilation systems
- animal carcases and contaminated vegetation
- dangerous buildings
- contaminated foodstuffs.

Box 8 contains an example of local authority involvement in remediation after an incident.

Legislation to remedy the effects of a chemical incident

Local authorities can use legislation either during an incident or in its immediate aftermath to achieve the following objectives:

- to provide systems to ensure that similar incidents do not occur;
- to ensure remediation of the damage to the environment and restoration of the environment to its previous condition; and
- to punish the perpetrator of the accident/incident.

Local authorities should be aware of other agencies with enforcement powers in different areas.

Box 8 Formaldehyde in water

The driver of a road tanker carrying formaldehyde lost control on the road. The tanker crashed through a barrier and rolled down a hill where it spilt its load over a residential property. Environmental health services were notified immediately by the emergency services. The residents were evacuated and the road was shut. A working group steered by EHPs was formed of representatives of the Highways Agency, the Environment Agency, the local health authority, CCDC and environmental consultants. The environmental consultants advised on remediation measures and health effects. EHPs were heavily involved in the incident response. Their involvement included:

• carrying out sampling of private water supplies. Five private water supplies were affected. Three of these had to use only bottled water until hydrological tests showed it was 'safe' or alternative boreholes had been sunk;

• keeping residents informed and liaising with the media. The council produced newsletters for local people who were affected;

• serving an abatement notice (EPA'90 S80) requiring remediation of the site which took two and a half years to complete;

• air and soil monitoring to verify the consultants' results and to ensure that a nuisance no longer existed.

Local authority enforced legislation

Nuisance provisions

The effect of the chemical incident may be a nuisance under the Environmental Protection Act 1990. The nuisance provisions are one of the oldest pieces of environmental protection legislation and deal with the nuisance or health impact of any one premises or land on another. Nuisance can be:

• smoke, fumes or gases from private dwellings;
• dust, steam, smell or other effluvia from industrial or trade premises;
• ponds, pools, ditches and watercourses;
• wells, tanks and cisterns; and
• accumulations or deposits of materials prejudicial to health or a nuisance.

Nuisance provisions are flexible, wide-ranging in their application and ideally suited to post-incident clear-up.

Atmospheric pollution

The site may be authorised/permitted under IPC/IPPC and the conditions may be breached. Action can be taken under the Environmental Protection Act 1990/Pollution Control and Prevention Act 1999 to ensure that the conditions are complied with.

The Clean Air Act 1993 deals with dark smoke from trade or industrial premises. The operator has a defence of inadvertent emission or that reasonable steps have been taken to prevent the emission.

Contaminated land

Contaminated land identification, assessment and remediation are controlled by the regime in the Environmental Protection Act 1990 as amended by the Environment Act 1995. These provisions allow for the remediation of land that is contaminated, i.e. poses significant risks to health. The process of agreeing remediation is a long one. The nuisance provisions, traditionally a speedier means to resolve small-scale acute contaminated land issues, are no longer available with the introduction of the contaminated land regime.

Health and safety at work

If an incident has arisen in a local authority enforced sector (the service sectors) there may be enforcement action under the Health and Safety at Work Act 1974 (HSWA) or regulations made under it. Chemical incidents/accidents are often the result of inadequate plant and equipment, inadequate maintenance, lack of training and supervision, lack of risk assessment and risk management and inadequate safety management. All of these are controlled by safety legislation. Regulations relating to risk assessment (The Management of Health and Safety at Work Regulations 1999) and chemicals (The Control of Substances Hazardous to Health Regulations 1999) are particularly relevant. The local authority can require that operations are made safe. If damage to the environment caused by the incident is causing an environmental health problem, action can also be taken under the HSWA.

Contamination of drainage systems

Public main sewerage systems are the responsibility of water and sewerage companies and are regulated mainly by the Environment Agency for any pollution of watercourses by their discharges. The effectiveness of private drainage systems is controlled by the local authority through the Building Act 1984. A system may become ineffective as a result of a chemical incident.

Food and drinking water contamination

Local authorities have powers to deal with food contaminated during preparation or sale under The Food Safety Act 1990 and regulations. Major contamination risks to food production in agriculture or elsewhere from the release of toxic chemicals and substances are controlled by emergency orders under the Food and Environment Protection Act 1985. Local authorities monitor drinking water quality in private supplies. In these private supplies drinking water standards are enforced by the local authority. In public water supplies, the Drinking Water Inspectorate ensures that standards are monitored and complied with.

Legislation enforced by other enforcement authorities

The Environment Agency enforces issues concerning

- contaminated watercourses
- waste on land including fly-tipping but not accumulations that may be prejudicial to health or a nuisance
- special contaminated land sites, i.e. those posing serious risk to health or pollution of watercourses (Environmental Protection Act 1990 as amended)

- discharges of radioactive substances to air, land or water (Radioactive Substances Act 1993)
- IPPC.

The Health and Safety Executive enforces issues concerning

- exposure of the public or workers to radioactivity (Ionising Radiation Regulation 1999)
- major hazard sites (Control of Major Accident Hazards Regulations 1999)
- poor safety management, risk assessment etc. in industrial/manufacturing/agricultural premises
- transport safety.

The Food Standards Agency and the Drinking Water Inspectorate will also be responsible for the enforcement of some food and drinking water safety legislation.

General considerations in managing remediation

The use of consultants

The local authority may lack the time, resources or skill to carry out part of the assessment of the impact of the incident or the development of options for remediation. If so, environmental consultants may be used. When using consultants

- the local authority's aims and objectives need to be clear;
- the aims and objectives of the sampling programme need to be agreed with the health authority and other interested agencies;
- the specification for the work needs to be clear;
- time-scales need to be agreed;
- the local authority must be satisfied that the consultants can provide a level of service that would be expected of an authority and do not expose the authority to potential liability;
- insurance and liability issues must be clear;
- the local authority must be satisfied with the health and safety management systems in the consultancy;
- the need for input from the local authority is not removed – the consultants must be managed and assisted with local information;
- the status of the final consultancy document needs to be agreed, i.e. whether it is a public document, limitations on its use;
- if remediation advice is requested, the nature and status of this advice must be defined.

Communicating with the public

This vital area sometimes appears to be less important once initial public concern has subsided and media interest wanes. However, it is vital that all those affected by the incident are kept actively informed of the progress of remediation. This could be achieved through regular public information material, e.g. newsletters, fact sheets, brochures, displays etc., briefings, public meetings or websites. Useful advice on techniques of communicating risk can be found in SNIFFER (1999).

Involving the public in risk management

For successful risk management it may be necessary not only to tell the public what the local authority is doing on its behalf but also to involve the public in decision-making. Where the public are suspicious about the extent of remediation and do not trust the industrial organisation involved or even the local authority, a traditional approach is unlikely to succeed. If it appears to the public that the local authority and the organisation that caused the pollution are agreeing action required for the protection of the public *behind closed doors*, it is very likely that the proposed remediation will be rejected by those it is designed to protect. Involving stakeholders in risk management is recommended by all major organisations advising on environmental health risk management. (See for instance Royal Commission on Environmental Pollution, 1998; National Academy of Sciences, 1996 and the Risk Commission, 1997a and 1997b.) There are practical difficulties in involving stakeholders, but local authorities have a long history of community involvement, especially in areas such as land-use planning.

When remediation is required by legislation, there are procedures by which the options for remediation are specified and agreed. These exist for contaminated land and under the nuisance provisions. In these instances, local authorities cannot involve the public and stakeholders in the generation of remediation options. What they can do, however, is

- while not compromising their role as an enforcer, be open and transparent in their dealings with the industrial organisations and other stakeholders;
- involve the stakeholders at the earliest opportunity;
- be open and transparent in communicating the local authority's objectives and the means of achieving them;
- listen to aspirations, objectives and expectations of the local stakeholders;
- be clear when the objectives of the local authority and the expectations of the local community do not meet and be transparent in explaining why;
- be realistic in estimating time-scales and the level of clean-up;
- listen to the local community and consider concerns that may appear irrational. Accept that most concerns expressed are genuine and deal with them in an open and transparent way.

21 Review and audit of response

Most chemical incidents need to be assessed and reviewed so that the sequence of events is understood and better strategies for the future can be developed. Debriefing, immediate or planned, may be important following an incident. It should be allowed for and resources allocated at the outset. Debriefing will be most helpful if all agencies are involved and lessons shared.

An audit of the response to a chemical incident is useful to determine its method and manner, as well as its appropriateness. The audit offers an opportunity to formalise lessons learnt and to incorporate them into the planning for any future event. Adequate documentation and report-writing must be available for audit.

Suitable audit measures include:

- early recognition and response to the incident;
- identification and control of the source of the incident and chemicals involved;
- identification and control of routes of contamination, i.e. environmental and person to person;
- comprehensive identification of those affected; and
- identification and elimination of risk factors that may have contributed to the incident.

Task 1: Preparation

Structure

- Was the local authority plan in place?
- Was the plan drawn up in consultation with the local health authority, emergency planning officer and the emergency services?
- Were the protocols for chemical incidents a natural extension of those used for the major disaster plan?
- Were the protocols for dealing with incidents capable of coping with events of different scales?
- Were additional resources, such as staff, rooms, communications equipment and computers available if needed?

Process

- Have individual roles been defined, e.g. the lead person for dealing with incidents?
- Did protocols cover nights, weekends and holidays?
- How often were the protocols updated?
- Did all those likely to be responsible for incident management understand their roles?

Outcome

- Has a chemical incident simulation exercise been carried out? If so, with what result?
- Was there an awareness of where plans were kept in different departments?

Task 2: Incident awareness

Structure

- Was there a system in place for the consultant in communicable disease control/consultant in public health medicine, GPs, emergency planning officers and emergency services, RSPU/chemical incident provider units to inform the environmental health services as soon as they recognised a chemical incident with health/environmental implications?
- Was there a system to ensure that EHPs recognised complaints and inquiries from the public as a possible chemical incident?
- Did this system incorporate chronic as well as acute exposure?

Process

- Did the environmental health complaint/inquiry systems record and monitor cases to allow detection of an abnormal distribution/clusters of complaints?

Outcome

- Was the average notification interval known for the different groups of informants?

Task 3: Initial investigation

Structure

- What information was sought in the initial investigation?
- Was there a pro-forma questionnaire available for use?
- Who collected the information, and on what authority?

Process

- What documentation was obtained and how maintained?
- What samples, if any, were taken?
- How was information from the field relayed to the coordinating centre?
- Were minutes distributed before the next meeting?

Outcome

- How long did it take to collect initial information?
- Did this information prove to be valid?
- What action was taken on the basis of the initial information?

Task 4: Incident control group

Structure

- Who called the group together and in what circumstances?
- Who chaired the incident control group? Was this agreed in advance?
- Did the composition of the group reflect appropriate and sufficient expertise for the management of the incident?
- Was a press officer designated?

Process

- Were all members of the group clear about their roles?
- Were meetings attended by all who were required?
- Were meetings minuted?

Outcome

- Were incident control group decisions acted upon fully?

Task 5: Risk assessment

Structure

- Were fate and transport of the chemicals identified?
- Was exposure information available/estimated?
- Were exposure histories available and used?

Process

- Was environmental sampling carried out?
- Was exposure and fate and transport modelling carried out?
- Were consultants used?
- Was a computer used for data handling and analysis?

Outcome

- Were the source of the incident and appropriate control options identified?

Task 6: Control and management procedures

Structure

- Were systems in place to ensure the correct documentation of evidence?
- Were systems in place to ensure that sampling protocols were complied with?
- Were systems in place to ensure that a range of control options were considered and the most appropriate adopted?

Process

- Did the procedures and protocols in place work successfully for the collection of evidence, sampling and remediation decision-making?

Outcome

- Was the evidence able to be used in a legal action or in an inquiry?
- How many of the samples taken were analysed?

Task 7: Communication

Structure

- Were communications procedures set out in the basic protocols?
- Did they include communications with local agencies, the media and the public?
- Were there facilities for a help line or assistance from NHS Direct?

Process

• Was the procedure followed?

Outcome

• Were there difficulties in managing the incident due to problems with communication?

Task 8: Completing an incident (recovery)

Structure

• Was there a procedure in place for declaring the incident over?
• Has the need for further monitoring and surveillance been identified and have procedures been put in place?

Process

• Was the incident documented or written up?
• Has legal action been considered?
• Has any action been taken to reduce the risk of a similar incident?

Outcome

• Were staff and other resources available for other work?
• Was the human distress resulting from the incident the least possible?
• Have any lessons learnt led to review of plans?
• Has any legal action been taken by or against the local authority? If so, what was the outcome?

Appendices

1 Sources of information

Emergency 24-hour telephone numbers: National Poisons Information Service

Belfast	02890 240503
Birmingham	0121 507 5588
Cardiff	029 20709901
Dublin	(+353) 1 837 9964 or (+353) 1 837 9966
Edinburgh	0131 536 2300
Leeds	0113 234 0715
London	0207 635 9191
Newcastle upon Tyne	0191 232 1525

Regional service provider units

London, South East, Eastern, North West, Trent, South and **West.** Health authorities in these regions are contracted with the Chemical Incident Response Service at the Medical Toxicology Unit, Guy's and St Thomas' Hospital Trust, Avonley Road, London SE14 5ER. Tel. 0207 771 5383 Fax. 0207 771 5382. 24-hour emergency via NPIS: Tel. 0207 635 9191. Fax. 0207 771 5309.

West Midlands. Health authorities in this region are contracted with the Chemical Hazard Management and Research Centre at the Institute of Public and Environmental Health, University of Birmingham, Birmingham B15 2TT. Tel. 0121 414 3985/6547 Fax. 0121 414 3827/3630. 24-hour emergency Tel. 0207 394 5112.

Northern and **Yorkshire Region.** Health authorities in this region are contracted with the Chemical Incident Service at The Department of Environmental and Occupational Medicine, The Medical School, University of Newcastle, Newcastle Upon Tyne NE2 4HH. Tel. 0191 2227195 or 0191 2303761. Fax. 0191 222 6442.

Scotland. Scottish Centre for Infection and Environmental Health at Clifton House, Clifton Place, Glasgow G3 7LN. Tel. 0141 300 1100. Fax. 0141 300 1170. Covers all health boards in Scotland.

Wales and **Northern Ireland.** Health authorities in these areas are contracted with the Chemical Incident Management Support Unit at University of Wales College of Medicine, Therapeutics and Toxicology Centre, Llandough Hospital, Cardiff CF64 2XX. Tel. 02920 709901. 24-hour emergency Tel. 029 20715278.

Public health laboratories

Belfast Regional Poisons Information Centre, Royal Victoria Hospital, Grosvenor Road, Belfast BT12 6BA. Tel. 02890 240503.

Birmingham Regional Laboratory for Toxicology, City Road Hospital, PO Box 293, Birmingham B18 7QH. Tel. 0121 507 4135.

Cardiff NPIS (Cardiff), Gwenwyn Ward, Llandough Hospital, Penarth, Vale of Glamorgan CF64 2XX. *Solvents, pesticides, drugs etc.*: Tel. 02920 711711 extension 5154/5197.

Glasgow Trace Elements Reference Laboratory, MacEwan Buildings, Glasgow Royal Infirmary, Glasgow G4 0SF. *Trace elements*: Tel. 0141 211 4256.

Guildford Trace Element Reference Centre, Department of Clinical Biochemistry & Clinical Nutrition, Robens Institute, University of Surrey, Guildford GU2 5XH. *Trace elements*: Tel. 01483 259220.

London Trace Metals Laboratory, Department of Clinical Biochemistry, King's College Hospital, Denmark Hill, London SE5 9RS. *Trace elements*: Tel. 0207 737 4000. Medical Toxicology Unit, New Cross, Avonley Road, London SE14 5ER. *Trace elements*: Tel. 0207 635 1060. *Solvents, pesticides, drugs etc.*: Tel. 0207 635 1050 or 0207 635 1058. *Non-biological material*: Tel. 0207 635 1060.

Newcastle upon Tyne Analytical Chemistry Unit, Department of Environmental and Occupational Medicine, Medical School, University of Newcastle, Newcastle upon Tyne NE2 4HH. *Non-biological material*: Tel. 0191 222 7015 or 0191 222 7255.

Southampton Trace Element Unit, Chemical Pathology Dept, Institute of Human Nutrition, Southampton General Hospital, Tremona Road, Southampton SO16 6YO. *Trace elements*: Tel. 02380 796419. Fax. 02380 796294.

Teddington Laboratory of the Government Chemist, Queens Road, Teddington, Middlesex TW11 0LY. *Non-biological material*: Tel. 0208 943 7000.

The health authority chemical advice provider or the National Focus should be able to advise on the battery of analyses each laboratory can perform. Contact the laboratories for estimates of cost and specific sampling instructions.

Public analyst laboratories

A network of 33 public analyst laboratories is subsumed under the umbrella of The Association of Public Analysts, Burlington House, Piccadilly, London W1V 0BN. Your local laboratory can be identified via the Yellow Pages under 'Public Analysts', 'Laboratory Facilities' or 'Chemists, Analytical and Research'.

Most laboratories serve more than one local authority. For a fee they will undertake chemical analyses of contaminants in air, soil, water, effluents, run-off, soil, spills, sediments, foods, ash and waste, contaminated land investigation and site surveys with risk and hazard assessment on behalf of statutory authorities on either an urgent or non-urgent basis.

Local

Local sources of information are the most useful in providing support and resources for chemical incident prevention and response. This list is not exhaustive but indicates the wide range of agencies which may have a role in a chemical incident:

- emergency services (police, fire and ambulance service)

- local health professionals, including general practitioners and hospital staff, in particular those in accident and emergency departments
- local government, including emergency planning officers, housing department and trading standards officers
- local officers or inspectors of the EA/SEPA, the HSE and the FSA.

National

Below are some of the relevant governmental departments and agencies. Other organisations, including university departments and institutes with medical toxicology, surveillance and environmental interests, voluntary agencies, societies and international agencies may also be useful. Any additional information required is likely to be available from the National Focus or the health authorities' regional service provider units.

Government departments and agencies

Communicable Disease Surveillance Centre 61 Colindale Avenue, London NW9 5EQ. Tel. 0208 200 6868.

Department of the Environment, Transport and the Regions Eland House, Bressenden Place, London SW1E 5DU. Tel. 0207 944 3000.

Department of Health 79 Whitehall, London SW1A 2NS. Tel. 0207 210 4850. (information service 10 a.m. to 4 p.m.) Switchboard: 0207 210 3000.

Department of Trade and Industry 1 Victoria Street, London SW1H OET. Tel. 0207 215 5000.

Drinking Water Inspectorate Ashdown House, 123 Victoria Street, London, SW1E 6DE. Tel. 0207 890 3000.

Environment Agency Rio House, Aztec West, Almondsbury, Bristol, BS3 4UD. Tel. 01454 624038 or 0207 863 8600.

Food Standards Agency – England Hannibal House, PO Box 30080, London SE1 6YA.

Food Standards Agency – Scotland St Magnus House, 6th Floor, 25 Guild Street, Aberdeen, AB11 8NJ.

Food Standards Agency – Wales 1st Floor, Southgate House, Wood Street, Cardiff, CF10 1EW.
FSA General inquiries 0845 9333111; Emergencies 0800 807060.

Health and Safety Executive Rose Court, 2 Southwark Bridge, London, SE1 9HS. Tel. 0207 717 6000.

Home Office 50 Queen Anne's Gate, London SW1H 9AT. Tel. 0207 273 4000.

Laboratory of the Government Chemist Queens Road, Teddington, Middlesex TW11 0LY. Tel. 0208 943 7000.

Medicines Control Agency Market Towers, 1 Nine Elms Lane, Vauxhall, London SW8 5NQ. Tel. 0207 273 0000 or 0207 273 0451.

Ministry of Defence Whitehall, London SW1A 2HB. Tel. 0207 218 9000.

Ministry of Agriculture, Fisheries and Food Nobel House, 17 Smith Square, London SW1P 3JR. Tel. 0207 2383000.

Ministry of Agriculture, Fisheries and Food: Veterinary Medicines Directorate Woodham Lane, New Haw, Addlestone, Weybridge KT15 3LS. Tel. 01932 336911.

National Chemical Emergency Centre Culham, Abingdon, Oxfordshire OX14 3ED. Tel. 01235 463060.

National Radiological Protection Board Chiltern, Didcot, Oxfordshire OX11 ORQ. Tel. 01235 831600. 24-hour emergency number: Tel. 01235 834590.

Office for National Statistics 1 Drummond Gate, London SW1V 2QQ. Tel. 0207 533 5257 (cancer stats.). General inquiries 0207 533 6363.

Scottish Centre for Infection and Environmental Health Clifton House, Clifton Place, Glasgow G3 7LM. Tel. 0141 300 1100.

Scottish Executive Tel. General inquiry line 08457741741, email ceu@scotland.gov.uk

National Assembly for Wales Tel. Public information 02920 898200, Main switchboard 01222 825111.

Other Agencies

British Association for Counselling 1 Regent Place, Rugby, Warwickshire CV21 2PJ. Tel. 01788 550899.

Health and Safety Executive: Pesticide Incident Appraisal Panel Rose Court, 2 Southwark Bridge, London SE1 9HS. Tel. 0207 717 6000.

Major Hazard Incident Data Service AEA Technology, Thomson House, Risley, Warrington WA3 6AT. Tel. 01925 254486.

Meteorological Office London Road, Bracknell, Berkshire, RG12 2SZ. Tel. 01344 420242.

Waste Management Information Bureau AEA Technology plc, F6, Culham, Abingdon, Oxfordshire OX14 3ED. Tel. 01235 463162. Fax. 01235 463004.

Water Research Centre Henley Road, Medmenham, Marlow, Buckinghamshire SL7 2HD. Tel. 01491 571531. Fax. 01491 579094.

University departments and institutes

Centre for Occupational Health, School of Epidemiology and Health Sciences, University of Manchester Stopford Building, Oxford Road, Manchester M13 9PT. Tel. 0161 275 5522.

Centres For Toxicology, Environmental Biotechnology, and Environmental Strategy, University of Surrey Guildford, Surrey GU2 5XH. Tel. 01483 300800.

The Chartered Institute of Environmental Health Chadwick Court, 15 Hatfields, London SE1 8DJ. Tel. 0207 928 6006.

Department of Environmental & Occupational Medicine and Epidemiology & Public Health, University of Newcastle The Medical School, Newcastle upon Tyne NE2 4HH. Tel. 0191 222 6000.

Department of Public Health and Environment and Institute of Occupational Health, University of Birmingham Edgbaston, Birmingham B15 2TT. Tel. 0121 414 6030.

Department of Environmental & Preventive Medicine St Bartholomew's Medical College, University of London, Wolfson Institute, Charterhouse Square, London EC1M 6BQ. Tel. 0207 982 6269.

Emergency Planning College Easingwold, Yorkshire YO61 3EG. Tel. 01347 821406.

Faculty of Occupational Medicine 6 St Andrew's Place, Regent's Park, London NW1 4LB. Tel. 0207 317 5890.

Institute for the Environment & Health, University of Leicester 94 Regent's Road, Leicester LE1 7DD. Tel. 0116 223 1600.

GKT Institute of Toxicology, King's College London 150 Stamford Street, Waterloo, London SE1 9NN. Tel. 0207 836 5454.

Life Sciences Department, King's College London 150 Stamford Street, Waterloo, London SE1 9NN. Tel. 0207 836 5454.

Robens Centre for Health Ergonomics, University of Surrey Guildford GU2 5XH. Tel. 01483 259203.

School of Applied Sciences, University of Wales Institute, Cardiff Institute of Higher Education Western Avenue, Llandaff, Cardiff CF5 2YB. Tel. 02920 416070.

Small Area Health Statistics Unit Department of Epidemiology and Public Health, Imperial College of Science, Technology and Medicine, Norfolk Place, London W2 1PG. Tel. 0207 589 5111.

South East Institute of Public Health Medical School, St Thomas' Hospital, London SE1 7EH. Tel. 0207 848 6606.

WHO Collaborating Centre for Environmental Assessment and Monitoring MARC, Life Sciences Department, King's College London SE1 9NN. Tel. 0207 836 5454.

WHO Collaborating Centre for Environmental Health Management Graham Jukes, Chartered Institute for Environmental Health, Chadwick Court, Hatfields, London SE1 8DJ. Tel. 0207 928 6006.

WHO Collaborating Centre for Health Aspects of Chemical Accidents, National Institute of Public Health and Environmental Protection Utrecht University Hospital, PO Box 85500, 3508 GA Utrecht, The Netherlands.

WHO Collaborating Centre for an International Clearing House for Major Chemical Incidents University of Wales Institute, Cardiff, Western Avenue, Llandaff, Cardiff CF5 2YB. Tel. 02920 416852.

Voluntary agencies

British Red Cross National Office, 9 Grosvenor Crescent, London SW1X 7EJ. Tel. 0207 235 5454.

St John Ambulance Brigade Headquarters, 1 Grosvenor Crescent, London SW1X 7EF. Tel. 0207 235 5231.

Samaritans Central London Office (admin. only), 46 Marshall Street, London W1V 1LR. Tel. 0207 439 1406.

Scottish Women's Royal Voluntary Service 44 Albany Street, Edinburgh EH1 3QR. Tel. 0131 558 8028.

Women's Royal Voluntary Service Milton Hill House, Milton Hill, Abingdon, Oxfordshire OX13 6AF. Tel. 01235 442900.

Societies

British Medical Association BMA House, Tavistock Square, London WC1H 9JP. Tel. 0207 387 4499.

British Occupational Hygiene Society Suite 2, Georgian House, Great Northern Road, Derby DE1 1LT. Tel. 01332 298101.

British Toxicology Society: Human Section Sub-Group Institute of Biology, 20 Queensbury Place, London SW7 2D2. Tel. 0207 581 8333.

European Association of Poisons Centres 20 Avenue Appia, CH-1211, Geneva 27, Switzerland. Tel. (+41) 22 791 21 11.

International Society of Toxicology Zentrum der Rechtsmedizin, Kennedy Allee 104, D 60596, Frankfurt, Germany.

Public Health Medicine Environment Group c/o Faculty of Public Health Medicine, 4 St Andrew's Place, Regent's Park, London NW1 4LB. Tel. 0207 933 0243.

Research Committee on Disasters University of Delaware, Newark DE1 9716, USA.

Royal Society of Chemistry Thomas Graham House, Science Park, Milton Road, Cambridge CB4 0WF. Tel. 01223 420066.

Society of Industrial Emergency Services Officers 11 Court House Gardens, Lower Cam, Dursley GL11 5LP. Tel. 01453 549225.

Society for Risk Analysis – Europe PO Box 247, 4102 Binningen 1, Switzerland. Tel. (+41) 61 422 13 70.

International agencies

Agency for Toxic Substances and Disease Registry 1600 Clifton Road, NE (E-28), Atlanta, GA 30333.

Centers for Disease Control and Prevention 1600 Clifton Road, NE, Atlanta, GA 30333.

International Programme on Chemical Safety (WHO/ILO/UNEP) 20 Avenue Appia, CH-1211, Geneva 27, Switzerland Tel. (+41) 22 791 21 11.

United Nations Environment Programme Industry And Environment Programme Activity Centre, 39–43 Quai André Citroën, 75739 Paris, France CEDEX 15. Tel. (+33) 1 44 37 14 50.

United Nations International Register of Potentially Toxic Chemicals (IRPTC) Case Postale 356, 15 chemin des Anemones, Chatelaine CH-1219, Geneva, Switzerland. Tel. (+41) 22 979 9111.

World Health Organisation Headquarters, 20 Avenue Appia, CH-1211, Geneva 27, Switzerland.

World Health Organisation Regional Office for Europe Scherfigsvej 8, DK 2100, Copenhagen, Denmark.

2   Sampling equipment and personal protective equipment

Personal protective clothing

- High-visibility protective overalls
- Hard hat
- Safety shoes or Wellington boots
- Ear plugs/ear defenders
- Safety glasses
- Disposable mask for nuisance dusts
- Heavy-duty chemically resistant gloves
- Disposable plastic gloves (powder-free)

General equipment

- Mobile telephone
- Map of the local area
- Emergency contact list
- Completed notification forms with basic information completed
- Site visit forms
- Disposable camera and film
- Official notebook and pens
- Torch
- Hazard tape
- Paper towels
- Tool kit
- Calculator
- Stationery including waterproof pens

Sampling equipment

- Small case for carrying samples
- Chain of custody sample forms
- Waterproof case for forms
- Triplicate bar codes for bottles or labels with space for name, time, date, site location
- PTFE tape for sealing bottles
- Sellotape
- 50 ml and 500 ml borosilicate glass bottles*
- 50 ml and 500 ml polythene bottles*

- Accelerant tins (available from Scenesafe) or wide-mouthed Teflon bottles
- Polythene or PTFE tape for sealing bags and glass bottles
- Polythene resealable sample bags
- Draeger tubes (CO, etc.)
- Grab bags and pump
- Sterile wipes
- Soil punch and hammer.

*Consult laboratory for compatibility with sample. As a general rule, glass bottles will interfere with analysis for metals, and polythene bottles with hydrocarbons.

All of the above equipment should be easily accessible and capable of being carried in a single hard case.

The case should be kept stocked at all times, and checked at regular intervals.

The names of laboratories and equipment suppliers can be found in the Environmental Data Services (ENDS) directory, Business Environment Directory, yellow pages or related publications.

A useful list of suppliers of sampling and monitoring equipment and their contact details can be found in I. Ashton and F. Gill (2000), *Monitoring for Health Hazards at Work*, 3rd edn, Blackwell Science.

3 Sampling protocols

The following issues must be considered in order to ensure that any environmental samples taken are reliable. They need to be incorporated into sampling protocols.

Chain of custody (audit trail)

Throughout the management of a chemical incident all phone calls, meetings, advice given and actions taken must be recorded. Everything should be documented in the same place, either in an official notebook or on the chain of custody form provided. Chain of custody applies specifically to sampling. It is essential to record where, when and by whom a sample is taken. This information should also be recorded on the sample bottle or bag (see labels and bar codes below). As the name suggests, this allows an incident or a sample to be followed.

Labels and bar codes

Labelling of samples is essential for both chain of custody and for validity of analytical results. Bar codes can be used but must be prepared in advance and accepted by the analytical laboratory. If bar codes are used they should be prepared in triplicate for sample, chain of custody form and a spare. Standard labels can also be used and a sample code generated for each sample. This code should be present on the lid, sample container, storage bags and on the chain of custody form. The form will provide all information relating to the sample, such as time taken, exact location, sampler, date. If standard labels are used a permanent waterproof marker must be used.

Contamination

Every effort should be made to reduce contamination of samples. The type of sample being taken will influence the effect contamination will have on results. For example, when analysing chemicals in water the levels of contamination are generally much lower than in soil and thus are more prone to sample bottle/equipment contamination. However, the same level of precaution should be exercised in all sampling to avoid cross-contamination. In some circumstances Teflon bottles are preferred over glass and plastic; however, as these are very expensive there is a tendency to clean and reuse them. This is not acceptable and would not be recommended practice.

- One-trip bottles and bags should be used.
- Disposable, powder-free gloves should be worn and changed each time sampling location is changed.
- Work from the least contaminated site to the most contaminated.
- Keep all equipment free of dirt, dust etc. that is likely to be contaminated and clean if necessary between samples.
- Keep equipment on a clean plastic sheet during sampling.
- Double-bag samples and store in sample case with separate compartments.

Duplicate samples and blanks

Duplicate samples should be taken so that multiple tests can be performed and stored for later use if necessary. There are two strategies proposed in the DETR guidelines (DETR, 1999), the second of which is preferable:

1. Bulk sample taken and split into sub-samples, then analysed (used to assess analytical precision).

2. Two discrete samples taken and analysed (used to assess total sampling precision).

Blank samples (controls) are essential because some chemicals are highly toxic at very low concentrations and so we need to be certain that contamination is reduced to a minimum. Blanks give an indication of extraneous matter introduced as a result of collection or treatment.

1. An analyte-free medium is prepared, e.g. triple distilled H_2O, acid–washed sand.

2. Put into identical container as is being used for sample.

3. Transport in the same way as samples. Keep closed throughout the sampling.

Background sampling

Background samples provide a reference point against which samples can be compared. These samples should be taken from an area adjacent to the site of interest, preferably with the same parameters. The method for determining where to take background samples depends upon the incident type and is detailed in DETR (1999).

Preservation, packaging and transport

Preservation of samples begins with the container to be used to collect the sample. It is essential to consult the laboratory not only about which container to use, but also what to treat it with. Sample containers should be filled almost to the top, with only enough room for change in temperature. This is most essential when organics are the suspected contaminant. Do not use bin liners for storing or carrying any samples. The recycled plastic they are made of contains a wide range of organic materials, plus a range of metals.

Packaging: once samples have been taken they should be double-bagged and then placed in the designated sample case. Background samples should **not** be stored in the same case. Cool-boxes may be required for samples containing organics and water samples.

Transporting: the most important point to note here is that samples should be delivered to the laboratory as quickly as possible: within 24 hours or less in most cases. Courier services should be used if hand delivery is not possible. If a sample is taken but analysis is not required immediately it should be sent to the laboratory for storage. Do not assume that a domestic refrigerator is suitable.

Quality assurance and control

Quality assurance is an umbrella term covering all stages of sampling, including quality control. Quality control is a term used to represent the technical activities carried out. In any sampling strategy there are many steps from planning through to analysis. Errors and uncertainties can be introduced through the process and in many cases cannot be avoided. The purpose of a quality assurance system is to ensure that these errors can be controlled and quantified. The use of standard operating procedures (SOPs) can ensure that the quality of analytical results is consistent. The laboratory will have its own SOPs for each method and the sampler should also follow specific guidelines.

Accredited laboratories

In order to ensure that a sample is subjected to the same levels of quality assurance an accredited laboratory must be chosen for analysis of samples. Accredited laboratories are generally more expensive but the results obtained can be used with confidence. Some times a technique cannot be carried out at an accredited laboratory, in which case another laboratory can be used. There are two bodies in the UK that may accredit laboratories:

- **UKAS**, which gives NAMAS accreditation
- **CPA**, which gives accreditation to health authorities and hospitals including laboratory analyses.

Qualities to consider when choosing a laboratory

- Accreditation
- 24 hour on-call service
- Experience with environmental sampling
- Willingness to provide advice over the phone.

The names of laboratories and equipment suppliers can be found in the Environmental Data Services (ENDS) directory, Business Environment Directory, yellow pages or related publications.

A useful list of suppliers of sampling and monitoring equipment and their contact details can be found in I. Ashton and F. Gill (2000), *Monitoring for Health Hazards at Work*, 3rd edn, Blackwell Science.

4 Information on hazardous chemicals

Information source	Available from	Tells you
Labelling and packaging information	Physical evidence. Information from emergency services, owner/operator of site or transport	Classification including physico-chemical, health and eco-toxicological data
Safety data sheets	Manufacturer	Identification information; occupational exposure levels; classification symbols; risk phrases; important hazards and adverse health effects; first aid, fire fighting, handling and storage information; exposure controls and PPE; physical and chemical properties; stability and reactivity information; toxicological and ecological information; disposal method; transport considerations; regulatory information
Criteria document summaries	Health and Safety Executive www.open.gov.uk/hse	Background information on the setting of an occupational exposure level including toxicological, epidemiological and exposure information. Control information is also included
TremCards	Driver of vehicle European Chemical Industry Council (CEFIC) http://cefic.be/activities/logistics	Basic information about the chemical and emergency instructions
RSPU/chemical incident provider units	Through your health authority or directly by local authority contract	Expert source of information on toxicological hazards and risk assessment. Units have extensive information, access to other information sources (such as those in Appendix 1) and advice and can tailor service to local needs
Environmental health criteria documents	World Health Organisation/ International Programme on Chemical Safety (IPCS)	Background toxicological and eco-toxicological information. Epidemiological information and global exposure data. Advice on standards

5 Deciding where to sample from a fire

This appendix has been taken from *Environmental Sampling after a Chemical Accident* (DETR, 1999). This document should be referred to when designing sampling protocols.

The method shown here is only for the initial sampling. When more time and resources are available, more complex methods can be used.

Limitations

- Some of the methods have simplified many complex calculations, so this method cannot cover all situations.
- It does not take into account complex terrain, e.g. mountains, that will alter the deposition pattern.
- It assumes no rain and assumes a roughness level of 100 cm which would correspond to an aerodynamically rough environment such as mixed suburban/industrial.

Table A5.1 gives the downwind distances at which to take samples from a fire. Figure A5.1 shows the locations graphically.

Table A5.1 Mark the downwind distances on the incident map

Fire Size	Try to sample at these distances downwind
Minor	2m, 10m, **25m**, 85m, 300m, 1km
Small	5m, 20m, **60m**, 200m, 850m, 3km, 10km
Medium	20m, 70m, **250m**, 850m, 3km, 10km
Large	50m, 180m, 350m, **600m**, 1km, 2km, 7.5km, 25km
Major	100m, 350m, 700m, **1.25km**, 2.3km, 4.25km, 15km, 50km

Notes: Single sample distances in bold. One sample is always taken very close to the source of the fire, since turbulence from the burning building or structures will enhance deposition close to the source. More samples are taken in large and major fires. Do not try to sample very close to the source if the fire is still burning! The other samples are taken at logarithmically spaced distances appropriate to the scale of the fire.

If the wind changes direction completely during the release, mark another series of downwind distances on the incident map for this direction as well and try to sample along that transect. If time is very short, concentrate on the transect where the wind has been prevailing.

For large fires it is worth taking samples upwind of the fire in addition to those samples collected as background.

Figure A5.1 Sampling locations following a fire

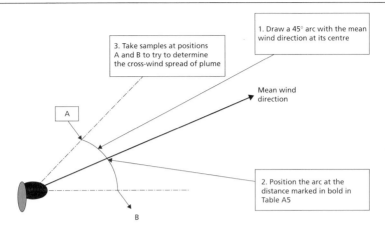

If you are short of time, take the sample nearest to the release and at the single sample distance only.

If it has been raining, sampling nearer to the source may be necessary.

Mark the sampling point on the incident map to assess the spread of contamination

Follow the instructions in Figure A5.1 to mark the positions (A and B) on the incident map where you should collect additional samples to assess the extent of cross-wind spread of contamination.

If the wind direction changes slightly during the release, widen the extent of the arc.

Using CHEMET

The CHEMET service may be able to identify for you the area of land that could have been contaminated based upon the meteorology during the accident. If you have access to this service (through the fire brigade), use the data to design your sampling plan. If the release is short (tens of minutes), CHEMET will not be able to predict the plume dispersal.

Decide on background sample locations

Background samples are necessary to give you a point of reference for the impact of the accident. They should be taken near to the time and location of the main sampling. Consideration should be given to the following points:

- For soil, there is often large geographical variability in concentrations over a scale of kilometres.
- For crops, residues of agricultural chemicals recently applied may skew the interpretation of the results.
- Sites downwind of major industrial sites or areas may have accumulated pollutants over a lengthy period, and levels in environmental media may be elevated.
- Some sites may already be contaminated with pollutants that have been released in an accident as a result of previous industrial activity.
- Your decisions during the accident could be wrong and you might sample in an area that has already been contaminated.

6   Deciding where to sample from a land spill

This appendix has been taken from *Environmental Sampling after a Chemical Accident* (DETR, 1999). This document should be referred to when designing sampling protocols.

This protocol will help you predict the area of the environment most heavily contaminated after a spill, and will aid in the design of a sampling campaign. It only focuses on the initial fast response required in an emergency. For longer-term sampling refer to DETR (1999).

Limitations

• The protocol does not cover solids.

If the contamination is visible, select several evenly spaced sampling points within the visibly contaminated area.

If not, try to decide the slope of the land, and the predominant direction in which the pollutant may have travelled. Mark the slope distances in Table A6.1 based upon the scale of the spill on an incident map. This will provide you with samples along a down-slope transect of the spill.

Table A6.1 Down-slope distances to sample based on scale of spill

Spill size	Try to sample at these distances down slope
Minor	At source, 1m, **2m**, 3m, 4m, 8m
Small	At source, 2m, 3m, **4m**, 5m, 7m, 10m
Medium	At source, 5m, 7m, **10m**, 15m, 25m, 40m
Large	At source, 50m, 75m, **100m**, 130m, 170m, 200m
Major	At source, 100m, 150m, **200m**, 300m, 400m

Notes: Single sample distances in bold. It may be hard to determine which direction the pollutant might have flowed in, or it may have flowed down two or more paths. Try to mark these on the incident map. If time is short, concentrate on the path you think the pollutant used.
Sample as near as you can to these locations.

If there is no clear slope, sample at the source and at points in three concentric rings as shown in Figure A6.1 and at distances shown in Table A6.2. This approach will also help to assess the spread of contamination.

Figure A6.1 Sampling locations following a spill to land

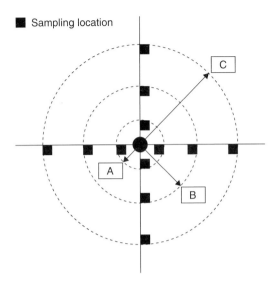

Table A6.2 Concentric distances away from source to sample based on scale of spill

| Spill size | Try to sample at these concentric distances from the source (and one at the source if possible) | | |
	A	B	C
Minor	1m	**2m**	4m
Small	2m	**4m**	8m
Medium	5m	**10m**	40m
Large	50m	**100m**	200m
Major	100m	**200m**	400m

7 Chemicals likely to be present in a fire

Fire type		CO	HCN	HCl	P_2O_5	Iso-cyanate	Irritants, e.g. acrolein	HF HBr	PAHs, e.g. benzene	NO_X	SO_2	NH_3	Particles
Rubber, tyres, belting	Emissions	+++	+	+	–	–	+++/++	–	++	+	++++	–	++
	Zone 2 risk	+-	+-	+	–	–	++/+	–	+-	+-	+++/+++	–	++
	Zone 3 risk	–	–	–	–	–	+	–	–	–	++	–	+
Petrol storage, e.g. petrol station	Emissions	++	–	–	–	–	++	–	+	–	–	–	+++
	Zone 2 risk	–	–	–	–	–	+	–	+-	–	–	–	++
	Zone 3 risk	–	–	–	–	–	–	–	–	–	–	–	+
Plastics factory/ warehouse	Emissions	+++	+++	+++	+	++	++	+	++	++	+	+	+++
	Zone 2 risk	+-	+-	++	–	++	++	+-	+-	+	+	+-	++
	Zone 3 risk	–	–	+	–	+	+	–	+-	–	–	–	+
Resins and adhesives	Emissions	+++	++	+	–	++	++	+	++	++	+	+	+++
	Zone 2 risk	+-	+-	+	–	++	++	+-	+-	+	+	+-	++
	Zone 3 risk	–	–	–	–	+	+	–	–	–	–	–	+
Paints and solvents	Emissions	+++	–	++	+	++	++	–	++	–	–	–	++
	Zone 2 risk	+-	–	+	–	++	+	–	+-	–	–	–	+
	Zone 3 risk	–	–	–	–	+	–	–	–	–	–	–	–
Upholstery – polyurethane	Emissions	+++	+++	+++	–	++	++	+	++	++	+	+	+++
	Zone 2 risk	+-	+-	++	–	++	++	+-	+-	+	+	+-	++
	Zone 3 risk	–	–	+	–	+	+	–	–	–	–	–	+

Fire type		CO	HCN	HCl	P_2O_5	Iso-cyanate	Irritants e.g. acrolein	HF HBr	PAHs, e.g. benzene	NO_X	SO_2	NH_3	Particles
Vegetation – forests	Emissions	+	-	-	-	-	+	-	+	+	-	-	+++
	Zone 2 risk	-	-	-	-	-	+	-	+-	+-	-	-	+-
	Zone 3 risk	-	-	-	-	-	-	-	-	-	-	-	-
Oil refineries, storage tanks	Emissions	+	-	-	-	-	++	-	+++	-	+	-	+++
	Zone 2 risk	-	-	-	-	-	++	-	+-	-	+	-	++
	Zone 3 risk	-	-	-	-	-	+	-	-	-	-	-	+
Waste tips	Emissions	-	+	+	-	+	++	+	+	+	+	+	++
	Zone 2 risk	-	+-	+	-	+	+	+-	+-	+-	+	+-	+
	Zone 3 risk	-	-	-	-	-	-	-	-	-	-	-	-
Pesticides and especially OP* stores	Emissions	+++	-	++	++	++	++	++	++	-	-	-	++
	Zone 2 risk	+-	-	++	++	++	+	+	+-	-	-	-	+
	Zone 3 risk	-	-	+	+	+	-	-	-	-	-	-	-
Phosphorus fires	Emissions	+++	-	+	+++	++	++	-	++	-	-	-	++
	Zone 2 risk	+-	-	+	++	++	+	-	+-	-	-	-	+
	Zone 3 risk	-	-	-	+	+	-	-	-	-	-	-	-
Chlorine	Emissions	}											
	Zone 2 risk	}N/A											
	Zone 3 risk	}											

* OP = organophospate

Source: Stroud (1996), *Smoke Toxins.* DH Health Advisory Group on Chemical Contamination Incidents.

8 Environmental/toxicological standards

Air

UK Air Quality Standards

Available from DETR, Eland House, Bressenden Place, London SW1E 5DU. Tel. 0207 944 3000.
Background information available in EPAQS (Expert Panel on Air Quality Standards) documents.
www.open.detr.gov.uk

Occupational exposure levels (OELs)

OELs are listed in EH40 Occupational Exposure Levels, issued annually by the HSE. Criteria document summaries and risk assessments are also available for particular chemicals from the HSE, Broad Lane, Sheffield, S3 7HQ. Tel. 0114289 2345.
www.open.gov.hse.uk

WHO Air Quality Guidelines

Published in WHO, *Air Quality Guidelines for Europe*. Reviewed regularly. www.who.org.int

Water

UK Drinking Water and Recreational Water Standards

Water standards are available from DETR, Eland House, Bressenden Place, London SW1E 5DU. Tel. 0207 944 3000.
www.open.detr.gov.uk

Land

Land standards are available from DETR, Eland House, Bressenden Place, London SW1E 5DU. Tel. 0207 944 3000.
www.open.detr.gov.uk

9 Initial desk-top assessment checklist

This checklist form will enable the initial desk-top assessment to be carried out. The information will come from the notifying organisation, from your existing local authority property files, from maps of the location, GIS, and any relevant public registers.

A GENERAL

Call received by   Position

Date   Time

Informant details

Name

Position

Address

Contact numbers

B ABOUT THE INCIDENT

Incident details

Type of event (see list below)

Date   Time

Type of premises

Company

Address

Postcode

Tel. number

Type of event

Fire   State of combustion in which inflammable material burns, producing heat, flames and often smoke.

Explosion   Violent release of energy resulting from a rapid chemical reaction, especially one that produces shock wave, loud noise, heat and light.

Waste   Inappropriate or unauthorised disposal of waste products, both domestic and industrial; seepage of waste products from waste disposal site to an adjacent site that leads to comtamination.

Water	Contamination of drinking water, oceans, rivers, lakes, estuaries, groundwater etc.
Food & drink	Contamination of any substance containing nutrients, such as carbohydrates, proteins and fats that is ingested for the purpose of generating energy and body tissue.
Medicine	Contamination of substances that are used to restore or preserve health.
Malicious act	Act motivated by wrongful, vicious or mischievous purpose.
Air	Contamination of the gases that we normally breathe.
Leak	Crack, hole or fault in a container or pipe leading to a release of material. Carbon monoxide exposures from blocked flues or faulty systems can be inserted here.
Spill	Act of disgorging contents from a container unintentionally.
Transport accident	Unforeseen event involving a vehicle used to transport goods or people.
Land	Contamination of the land surface of the earth that is composed of disintegrated rock particles, humus, water and air.

What is known to have occurred?

Give a description of the incident and name/contact details of other agencies that are already involved.

_____

_____

_____

_____

_____

_____

C POTENTIAL EXPOSED POPULATION

From a map, determine whether there is a human population near to the incident site.

Has anyone been exposed to the chemicals?

Yes ☐   No ☐   Don't know ☐

Information about casualties or exposed persons and their management

Exposed
Symptomatic
Casualties
Deaths

If you don't know who has been exposed, is there the potential for exposure of the population?

Yes ☐   No ☐   Don't know ☐

If NO, explain why.

_____

_____

If YES or **DON'T KNOW**, obtain more information either by reference to files, other agencies, informants or through a SITE VISIT.

From maps or local information, what is the size of the potentially exposed local population? Are there any vulnerable populations, e.g. schoolchildren, the elderly etc.?

_____

_____

D THE EXTENT OF CONTAMINATION

Weather conditions (Please give details of prevailing conditions, e.g. dry, overcast, windy with direction if known)

_____

_____

Is weather likely to change?

_____

_____

Information from CHEMET

_____

_____

E MAJOR INCIDENT?

If Yes,   has a major incident been declared? Yes ☐   No ☐

If Yes,   When? _____

               By whom? _____

               Position? _____

               Meet at _____

Date

Time

Lead person

Name

Organisation

Position

Contact number

F NATURE OF CHEMICALS INVOLVED

What chemicals are present or likely to be present?

Are they hazardous to health?

IF YOU DON'T KNOW the answer to the above questions, either conduct inquiries to obtain the information or carry out a SITE VISIT.

Chemical substances involved

Substance 1

Name(s)

Confirmed/suspected?

Amount (kg)

UN No.

Manufacturer CAS No.

Physical state of chemical

Radioactive?   Yes ☐   No ☐

Affecting air/water/food/soil/not known/other (please specify)?

Substance 2

Name(s)

Confirmed/suspected?

Amount (kg)

UN No.

Manufacturer CAS No.

Physical state of chemical

Radioactive?   Yes ☐   No ☐

Affecting air/water/food/soil/not known/other (please specify)?

G DOES A PLAUSIBLE SOURCE–PATH–RECEPTOR LINKAGE EXIST?

No ☐   If not, explain why

Yes ☐   SITE VISIT REQUIRED

Don't know ☐   SITE VISIT REQUIRED

H ACTION REQUIRED

Detailed log

Site visit

Refer to local major incident plan

Incident control team

Liaison (note name of contact, contact number, date, time and reason for contact):

Organisation/dept.

Emergency services

Fire

Police

Ambulance

Health authority

CCDC

DPH

EPO

GM

Clerical

Media

Other 1

Other 2

Local authority

Emergency planning

Education

Highways

Social services

Housing

Media liaison

Specialist centres

Regional service provider unit

NPIS

SCIEH

National Focus

HAGGCI

Voluntary agencies

Others

Continuing action needed?   Yes ☐   No ☐

If no, why not?

10 Site visit pro forma

Name of visiting officer

Date   Time

Pre-visit checklist

Have you got the appropriate

- Safety equipment and PPE?
- Sampling and monitoring equipment?
- Protocols, checklists and forms?
- Map of incident area/location?
- Torch, stationery etc?

Have your local authority safety procedures been followed?

- Have you got mobile phones, pagers etc?
- Does your authority (and others involved in incident management) know of your whereabouts?
- Are you following safety procedures as per the risk assessment conducted under the Management of Health and Safety at Work Regulations?

On arrival at the scene

- Report to emergency service commander on the scene.
- Ascertain what emergency services require of you.
- Follow emergency services safety instructions.
- Gain as much information as possible from the emergency services or fire brigade hazardous materials officer.

Some of the information on the site visits form may be available before the visit. Complete as much as you can before going on site, but verify the information during the visit.

A DESCRIPTION OF INCIDENT

What has happened?

Give detailed description of the event that led to the release of chemicals.

How much chemical, what type, nature of release, time period of release, action taken by operators and emergency services etc.

Contact details of witnesses

_____

_____

_____

_____

What is the present scene? – visual observations

Any information that may assist in the identification of the chemical – packaging, labelling, the nature of the process conducted etc.

_____

_____

_____

_____

Complete the visual observation form (see Table A10.1 on page 125).

Take photographs, sketches.

B DETAILS OF THE SITE

How big is the site of the incident?

_____

_____

Postcode or Map reference:

_____

_____

What is the topography?

_____

_____

_____

_____

What activities are carried out on the site?

_____

_____

_____

_____

What is known about the history of the site and adjacent land?

_____

_____

_____

_____

C DETAILS OF THE RELEASE

Release to air

As a result of a fire?   Yes ☐   No ☐

CHEMET plume prediction?   Yes ☐   No ☐

Release to land

Liquid/solid?

Is there visible contamination?   Yes ☐   No ☐

What is the soil type?

Details of slope of ground and topography?

_____

_____

_____

_____

Are there any watercourses nearby?   Yes ☐   No ☐

Are there any aquifers on site or nearby? Yes ☐   No ☐

Release to water

Release to drains, sewers, recreational waters, rivers, drinking water supplies?

_____

_____

_____

_____

Is fire-water run-off likely to affect these water sources?

_____

_____

Weather Conditions?

Wind direction, speed, temperature, pressure, humidity, rainfall etc.

_____

_____

_____

_____

D WHAT IS THE CHEMICAL RELEASED AND WHAT IS THE NATURE OF THE HAZARD?

Is the chemical identified?   Yes ☐   No ☐

If Yes, are safety data sheets available?   Yes ☐   No ☐

Nature of hazards

Complete the following.

Use information sources on chemicals (Appendix 4) or toxicology (Appendix 1) or the health authority will have access to RSPU and toxicological databases.

Substance 1

Name(s) _____

Confirmed/suspected? _____

Amount (kg) _____

UN No. _____

Manufacturer CAS No. _____

_____

_____

Physical state of chemical

Radioactive?   Yes ☐   No ☐

Affecting air/water/food/soil/not known/other (please specify)?

Hazards?

Controls

Substance 2

Name(s)

Confirmed/suspected?

Amount (kg)

UN No.

Manufacturer CAS No.

Physical state of chemical

Radioactive?   Yes ☐   No ☐

Affecting air/water/food/soil/not known/other (please specify)?

Hazards?

Controls

If No,

Environmental sampling

If the chemical is unknown, take a sample of air, water, soil or deposit. For identification purposes, a spot/grab sample may be adequate.

FOLLOW THE APPROPRIATE SAMPLING PROTOCOL FOR THE MEDIA AFFECTED BY THE RELEASE

E HOW MUCH CHEMICAL HAS BEEN RELEASED?

Do the emergency services or the site operator know?   Yes ☐   No ☐

Have you any visual observations that might assist in determining the amount of release?

_____

_____

If it is not possible to obtain quantitative data, give a qualitative estimate of the amount of chemical released.

_____

_____

_____

_____

What is the basis of this estimate?

_____

_____

_____

_____

Environmental sampling

To determine the extent of the release, environmental sampling may be necessary. Determine the suspected spread of pollution (use Appendices 5 and 6).

FOLLOW THE APPROPRIATE SAMPLING PROTOCOL FOR THE MEDIA AFFECTED BY THE RELEASE

F IS THE POPULATION EXPOSED TO THE CONTAMINANT?

Mark out the possible spread of the contaminant and the location of populations on an incident map.

G IS THERE A SOURCE–PATH–RECEPTOR LINKAGE?

Yes ☐   No ☐   Don't know ☐

If No, then no emergency remedial action is required.

If Yes, is there anything that could be done immediately to prevent the exposure of the local population, e.g. removal of the hazard, containment of the hazard?

_____

_____

_____

_____

_____

If so, what action?

_____

_____

_____

_____

Is it practicable and feasible to take such action?   Yes ☐   No ☐

If Yes, ensure such action is taken.

Taken when

_____

_____

_____

_____

By whom?

_____

_____

If No, explain why such action is not feasible.

_____

_____

_____

_____

If No, and action cannot be taken quickly and easily to prevent the release, the degree of exposure of the local population needs to be established.

H WHAT CONCENTRATIONS ARE THE POPULATION EXPOSED TO?

Visual observations?

Complete the visual observation form (see Table A10.1 on page 125).

Environmental sampling

To compare with exposure standards the sampling needs to be representative.

FOLLOW THE APPROPRIATE SAMPLING PROTOCOL FOR THE MEDIA AFFECTED BY THE RELEASE

I IMMEDIATE ACTION REQUIRED

- Action to prevent the hazard affecting the population if feasible.
- If environmental sampling is necessary but equipment not available, contact environmental consultant.
- If prevention not possible, carry out qualitative risk assessment with the health authority.
- If there is a risk to health, take immediate management action.
- Contact appropriate enforcement agency (HSE, EA, FSA, DWI).
- Contact water companies

J IMMEDIATE MANAGEMENT OPTIONS

Advice to public?

Yes ☐   No ☐   Deferred ☐

Date required _____ Time required _____

Method   Press statement ☐   Leaflet ☐   Vans ☐   GP ☐

Other(s) ☐

Protection of public

Is a decision on sheltering/evacuation needed?   Yes ☐   No ☐

Has it been made?   Yes ☐   No ☐

What was it? _____

Zone description _____

Time _____

Who made it? _____

Name _____

Position _____

Contact no. _____

How is it being issued? _____

Table A10.1 Visual observations/odour observation form

Medium to observe	Things to record	Observations
Water	Colour of water	
	Surface film?	
	Surface foam?	
	Dead fish or animals?	
	Turbidity of water	
	Odour?	
Air	Colour of plume	
	Size and shape of plume	
	Extent of plume	
	Size of particulates	
	Odour?	
Land/vegetation	Appearance of deposition	
	Pollution indicators present?	
	Damage to vegetation?	
	Dead/dying animals?	
	Odour?	

Table A10.2 may provide a useful guideline for predicting the likely chemical from the odour. However, note that there are many other chemicals that may also have a similar odour. Thus the table must be used simply as a preliminary tool.

Table A10.2 Predicting chemical from odour

Odour	Possible chemicals responsible for odour
Ammonical	Ammonia, trimethylamine
Burnt rubber	Diphenyl sulphide
Decayed cabbage	Ethyl mercaptan, methyl mercaptan
Decayed vegetables	Carbon disulphide, methyl sulphide, dimethyl sulphide
Earthy	Ethyl acrylate
Faecal	Skatole
Fishy	Methylamine, dimethylamine, trimethylamine
Medicinal	Phenol, chlorophenol
Onion, mustard	Phosphine
Putrid, decay	Ethyl mercaptan, thiophenol
Rotten eggs	Hydrogen sulphide
Sharp, pungent	Ammonia, sulphur dioxide
Skunk, rancid	Crotyl mercaptan, thiocresol
Sweaty	Butyric acid, valeric acid
Sweet	Acetylaldehyde

Source: DETR (1999).

11 Checklist for communicating health risks

This checklist is from the Department of Health publication, *Communicating about Risks to Public Health: Pointers to Good Practice* (DH, 1999).

Scanning and reacting

1. This checklist can be used:
   - for **scanning** to help identify difficult cases and prioritise attention
   - to guide reaction to **unforeseen incidents**.

   In both cases, communication should be considered as early as possible, as an integral part of risk assessment and management.

Anticipating public impact

2. Public responses to risks will be influenced by:
   - **fright factors** (see Box 6, Chapter 15)
   - **media triggers** (see Box 7, Chapter 16)

   A high score on either list indicates a need for particular care. A high score on both should alert you to a possible high-profile scare. Conversely, it will be difficult to direct public attention to low-scoring risks.

3. **'Indirect' effects** are commonly caused by people's responses to the original risk. Have possible economic, social and political consequences been considered?

Planning a communication strategy

4. Are the aims of communicating clear? Note that objectives should be:
   - **agreed internally** between relevant staff with different responsibilities (e.g. technical advisers, press staff)
   - **prioritised**, so that the most important aim is agreed.

5. Have the **key stakeholders** been identified? These will usually include both intended audiences and others who may react.

6. What is known (or is being assumed) about **how different stakeholders perceive the issue?** Does this require further investigation? What are the likely levels of **trust,** and what can be done to influence this?

7. Can the proposed message be seen as **inconsistent with previous messages** or with other policies? How can this be avoided or, failing that, explained?

8. Are mechanisms in place for keeping all the above **under review?**

The process of communication

9. Is there a checklist of **whom to involve** at each stage of information release? If so, is it in use?

10. In deciding how and when to involve external stakeholders:

- are decisions being considered as early as possible, and taken **on a consistent and defensible basis?**

- are any **decisions against openness** both necessary and clearly explained? Have mechanisms for involvement been **made clear to others?**

11. **What other actions are being taken** to deal with the risk in question? Do these support or undermine the intended communication? What overall impression is being conveyed?

Content of communication

12. Do statements attend to likely **values of the audiences** (e.g. perceived fairness, or need to vent anger), as well as providing factual information? Is the emotional tone appropriate to this?

13. Have **uncertainties** in scientific assessments been acknowledged?

14. In any statements about **probabilities:**

- if **relative risks** are given, is the 'baseline' risk made clear?

- do **risk comparisons** serve to illuminate alternative options? Could any comparisons appear unfair or flippant?

15. Have **framing effects** of wording (e.g. 'lives lost' versus 'lives saved') been considered?

Monitoring of decisions and outcomes

16. Are procedures in place to **monitor** actions and results?

17. Are there mechanisms for **reviewing** strategy and outcomes, and **disseminating** lessons for future practice?

Further analysis

18. Might **further analysis** be appropriate? If so, has assistance been sought?

12 Risk assessment information

Risk assessment information tends to originate in the United States. Although high-quality, some US risk assessment information is not applicable to the UK because of differing legal, political and social systems. Below is a list of information sources that are applicable to the UK.

Websites

A database of risk assessment resources including

- software,
- databases,
- organisations involved in risk assessment,
- books and journals,
- consultancies and directories, and
- websites

at http:// service.eea.eu.int/environwindows/riskindex.shtml.

List of air dispersion models at
http://www.wrc.noaa.gov/sites/hazmat/cameo/aloha.html.

An inventory of Information Sources on Chemicals at
http://irptc.unep.ch/irptc/invent/igo/html.

A network of risk sites and information at http://www.riskworld.com.

Books

There are huge numbers of books on risk assessment. The following are a few good introductory texts. Further information can be found on the European Environment Agency website.

Royal Society (1992), *Risk Analysis, Perception and Management*, Royal Society

Covello, V. and Merkhofer, M. (1994), *Risk Assessment Methods: Approaches for Assessing Health and Environmental Risks*, Plenum Publishing

van Leewen, C. and Hermens, J. (1995), *Risk Assessment of Chemicals – An Introduction*, Kluwer Academic Publishers

Department of the Environment, Transport and the Regions (2000), *Risk Assessment and Management for Environmental Protection*, The Stationery Office

Pitblado, R., Stricoff, S., Bartell. S. and Kolluru, R. (1996), *Risk Assessment and Management Handbook: For Environmental, Health and Safety Professionals*, McGraw-Hill

The Risk Commission (The Presidential/Congressional Commission on Risk Assessment and Risk Management) (1997), *Framework for Environmental Health Risk Management*, The Presidential/Congressional Commission on Risk Assessment and Risk Management, Washington, DC

The Risk Commission (The Presidential/Congressional Commission on Risk Assessment and Risk Management) (1997), *Risk Assessment and Risk Management in Regulatory Decision-Making*, The Presidential/Congressional Commission on Risk Assessment and Risk Management, Washington, DC

Fairman, R., Mead, C. and Williams, W.P. (1998), *Environmental Risk Assessment: Approaches, Experiences and Information Sources*, European Environment Agency, Copenhagen

Royal Commission on Environmental Pollution (1998), *21st Report Setting Environmental Standards*, The Stationery Office

Royal Society (1998), *Risk and Public Policy*, Royal Society

Department of Health (1999), *Communicating about Risks to Public Health: Pointers to Good Practice*, Department of Health, London

Databases and Software

For databases on toxicological hazards, miscellaneous biological and industrial hazards and software models (risk assessment, exposure assessment, fate and transport of chemicals and hazard identification/release assessment), see http:// service.eea.eu.int/environwindows/riskindex.shtml.

13 Checklist to facilitate evacuation/ sheltering decisions

Whether to evacuate or shelter will be a multi-agency decision. This is a checklist of the issues that need to be considered by the team.

Evacuation or Sheltering?

1. Is the substance harmful to the public?
   - Highly toxic/toxic/irritant/non–irritant
   - Short–term/long–term effects
   - Explosive/non–explosive
2. Will the public be exposed?
   - Substance contained
   - Potential for release
   - Capable of dispersal via wind, rain, etc.
   - Public in path of projected dispersal route
   - Distance, height of plume, meteorological conditions, stability of weather conditions
3. Will dilution factors minimise the risk?
4. When will the public be exposed (time of day)?
   - Already exposed
   - Imminently
   - Not for a few hours
5. How long will the exposure last?
   - Few minutes
   - Hours
   - Days
   - Months
   - Years

Criteria for returning home after evacuation

1. Incident under control and not expected to return.
2. The residential premises considered safe for residents.
3. Where necessary, environmental sampling and analyses to provide risk assessment information in residential premises.
4. Where necessary, discuss results with a medical toxicologist from an RSPU.
5. Evacuation leaflet providing advice on the situation and actions on returning, such as opening windows and doors to vent premises for appropriate period of time.
6. Advice about whom to contact if any ill-health develops, such as NHS Direct, GP or local Accident and Emergency Department.

Bibliography

Agency for Toxic Substances and Disease Registry (1997) *Hazardous Substances Emergency Events Surevillance*, Atlanta, GA: US Department of Health and Human Services.

Avon Health Authority (2000) *Major Incident Reference Plan*, Bristol: Avon Health Authority.

Bedfordshire Emergency Services Major Incident Committee and Hertfordshire Emergency Services Major Incident Committee (1997) *Local Authority Environmental Health Toolkit for Handling Chemical Incidents*, Bedford: BCCEP.

British Medical Association (1998) *Health and Environmental Impact Assessment*, London: Earthscan Publications.

Chartered Institute of Environmental Health (2000) *The Role of EHOs in Emergency Planning: Professional Guidance*, London: CIEH.

Chemical Hazard Management and Research Centre (1999) *Annual Report 1998/9*, Birmingham: University of Birmingham, Department of Public Health and Epidemiology.

Commission of the European Communities (1993a) 'Comm 93/67 Principles of risk assessment', OJ L227 08.09.93.

Commission of the European Communities (1993b) 'Regulation on the evaluation and control of existing substances', OJ L 84 5.4.93.

Dalkin, J. (1994) 'A media plan is a must', *Civil Protection*, **31**, 12–13.

Dardamissis, E. and McDonald P. (2000) 'Health decisions and information-taken without involving the Health Authority', *Chemical Incident Report*, 17, pp.14–15.

Department of the Environment (1988) *Survey of Derelict Land in England*, London: HMSO.

Department of the Environment/Department of Health (1996) *United Kingdom Environmental Health Action Plan*, Cm 3323, London: The Stationery Office.

Department of the Environment, Transport and the Regions (1999) *Environmental Sampling after a Chemical Accident*, London: The Stationery Office.

Department of the Environment, Transport and the Regions (2000) *Risk Assessment and Management for Environmental Protection*, London: The Stationery Office.

Department of Health (1993) 'Arrangements to Deal with Health Aspects of Chemical Incidents', National Health Service Management Executive Health Service Guidance HSG (93) 38, London: Department of Health.

Department of Health (1998) 'Planning for Major Incidents', National Health Service Management Executive Health Service Guidance, London: Department of Health.

Department of Health (1999) *Communicating about Risks to Public Health: Pointers to Good Practice*, London: Department of Health.

Fairman, R. (2000) 'Risk Assessment in Environmental Health Regulation', *Environmental Health Journal*, **108/9**.

Fairman, R., Mead, C. and Williams, W.P. (1998) *Environmental Risk Assessment: Approaches, Experiences and Information Sources*, Copenhagen: European Environment Agency.

Fairman, R. and Waterworth, E. (2001) *The preparedness of local authorities to deal with chemical incidents,* in preparation.

Farrow, C., Wheeler, H., Bates, N. and Murray, V. (2000) *The Chemical Incident Management Handbook*, London: The Stationery Office.

Fowle, S., Constantine, C., Fone, D. and McCloskey, B. (1996) 'An epidemiological study after a water contamination incident near Worcester, England in April 1994', *Journal of Epidemiology and Community Health*, **50** (1), pp.18–23.

Fisher, J., Morgan-Jones, D., Murray, V. and Davies, G. (1999) *Chemical Incident Management for Accident and Emergency Clinicians*, London: The Stationery Office.

Haigh, N. (2000) *Manual of Environmental Policy*, London: Institute for European Environmental Policy.

Institute of Environment and Health (1999) *Risk Assessment Approaches used by the UK Government for Evaluation Human Health Effects of Chemicals*, Leicester: Institute of Environment and Health.

Irwin, D., Cromie, D. and Murray, V. (1999) *Chemical Incident Management for Public Health Physicians*, London: The Stationery Office.

Hall, D. J. and Kukadia (1993) *Background to the HMIP Guidelines on Discharge Stack Heights for Polluting Emissions*, Stevenage: Warren Spring Laboratory.

Health and Safety Executive (1989) *Risk Criteria for Land-use Planning in the Vicinity of Major Industrial Hazards*, London: HMSO.

Health and Safety Executive (1994) *Arrangements for Responding to Nuclear Emergencies*, London: HMSO.

Health and Safety/Local Authority Enforcement Liaison Committee (2000) *Circular 20/2: Major Incident Response Procedures*, London: HMSO.

Hill, P. and O'Sullivan, D. (1992) *Survey of the arrangement for the identification and investigation of incidents of acute exposure of the public to toxic substances*, London: NHS Executive.

Home Office (1997) *Dealing with Disaster*, Liverpool: Brodie Publishing.

International Programme on Chemical Safety (1999) *Public Health and Chemical Incidents*, Wales: WHO Collaborating Centre for an International Centre for Major Chemical Incidents.

Last, J. (1982) 'Towards a dictionary of epidemiological terms', *International Journal of Epidemiology*, **11** (2), pp.188–9.

LB Southwark (1999) *Emergency Response Plan*, London: LB Southwark.

Lancashire County Council (2000) *Chemical Incident Plan*, Lancashire: Lancashire County Council.

National Academy of Sciences (1996) *Understanding Risk: Risk Decisions in a Democratic Society*, Washington DC: NAS.

Murray, V. (2000) 'Sheltering versus evacuation', *Chemical Incident Report*, **17**, pp.2–3.

Organisation for Economic Co-operation and Development (1992) *Guiding Principles for Chemical Accident Prevention, Preparedness and Response*, Paris: OECD.

Parker, N. and Baldwin, D. (1994) 'Warning the public in an emergency', *Civil Protection*, **33**, (10).

Palmer, S. (2000) National Focus, personal communication.

The Risk Commission (The Presidential/Congressional Commission on Risk Assessment and Risk Management) (1997a) *Framework for Environmental Health Risk Management*, Washington DC: The Presidential/Congressional Commission on Risk Assessment and Risk Management.

The Risk Commission (The Presidential/Congressional Commission on Risk Assessment and Risk Management) (1997b) *Risk Assessment and Risk Management in Regulatory Decision-Making*, Washington DC: The Presidential/Congressional Commission on Risk Assessment and Risk Management.

Royal Commission on Environmental Pollution (1998) *21st Report Setting Environmental Standards*, London: The Stationery Office.

SNIFFER (1999) *Communicating Understanding of Contaminated Land Risks*, SNIFFER (Scotland and Northern Ireland Forum For Environmental Research)/Environment Agency/Scottish Environmental Protection Agency, Environment and Heritage Service.

Stark, C., Christie, P. and Marr, C. (1994) 'Run an emergency help line', *British Medical Journal*, **309**, pp.44–5.

Waterworth, E. and Fairman, R. (2000) 'What role do local authorities have in chemical incidents?', *Environmental Health Journal*, **108**, (10).

http://www.natfocus.uwic.ac.uk/survfram.htm accessed November 2000.

Index

Note: page numbers in *italics* refer to figures and tables

**Index compiled by
Jill Halliday**

Printed in the United Kingdom for The Stationery Office
05/01 627586 19585 TJ003629